Armed with his secrets fro ...ie inside, Elton, hꙍ
internet marketing since 1997. As a public spe
Entrepreneur, mentor and one who has 'worn th
internet is both amusing and enlightening. More importantly, ne is pu.......
both saving and making you money through internet marketing. His approach is very
firmly centred on Profit and return on Investment.

If you are looking for a 'pretty website', you will hate this book. If you need to make
sure you get a return on the investment you are about to pay out (for the first time or
once again), you categorically need this book. It is about to save you the cover price
time and time again. Return on Investment starts here...

ISBN No: 978-0-9569110-0-1
Published by Urban Media Direct
May 2011
www.urbanmedia.co.uk/Direct
First Published 2011 in t 00053506

Contents

Introduction   **6**

De-mystifying the terminology   **11**

Before we begin   **36**

Plan, Plan and Plan   *37*

    Your Avatar   38

    Your specific Niche   39

    Start with the end in mind   41

Know Your Numbers   *42*

    Lifetime Customer Value (LCV)   43

    The Compound Effect   44

    Cost of Acquisition   45

Think it Through   *46*

    When is a website not a website?   46

    To sell or not to sell   47

    EBay Shops and Amazon Seller   49

    DIY or hire a PRO   50

    Google & Social Media are not the answer!   51

    PC, Mac or Smartphone?   52

    Building a tribe   53

Attract   **58**

Keyphrase research   *59*

Competitor analysis   *62*

Natural optimisation   *65*

    The Search Engine Algorithm   65

    On Page   67

Off Page 72

Paid advertising *77*

Social Media *81*

Creating an integrated campaign 81

Watch the time! 82

Recycle your material 83

Overview of your options 84

Facebook 84

LinkedIn 87

Twitter 91

YouTube 94

Flickr 96

Slideshare 98

Blogging 100

Convert **107**

Navigation *108*

Copy *109*

Layout *112*

Call to action *114*

Value chain *115*

Testimonials = increased sales *116*

What's on offer? *119*

Your 100% Satisfaction Guarantee *120*

Video is the new black *123*

Advertising on your site (Adsense) *124*

Affiliate Schemes 126

Measure **130**

Google Analytics 131

Deciding what is important 132

Assigning Actions & Responsibilities 133

Bounce rate 134

Referred source 135

Visits 136

Time on Site 137

Goal conversions 138

Continued conversations **143**

Mass Mail is dead (if it ever lived!) 145

Email newsletter 146

Told/Sold (gap analysis) 148

Auto Responders 152

Mail Blasts 155

Summary 155

Appointing a partner **160**

Cost and Expectations 162

Their testimonials 167

Their guarantee 168

The Beginning.... **172**

Foreword

Right at this very moment, hundreds of thousands, possibly millions of eager businesses are struggling with a sickness called "marketing myopia". This is characterized by a lack of ability to see the big picture of maximizing internet marketing, failure to perceive how this channel truly works, and inability to have long term business vision.

In short, the majority of businesses have SOME idea of how to succeed, but they never truly get a grasp of the entire picture of how to make it big by leveraging the power of the internet.

There are many "gurus" out there teaching unproven concepts and theories to others with the sole aim of raking in huge profits for themselves. But it rarely works. Very often, when the blind lead the blind, both fall into the ditch. The only way for you to get cured of this marketing myopia (short sightedness) is for someone to open your eyes to the realities of the online business world. In short, every business owner needs to know the FULL story of internet marketing! Elton is the man with the vision to help you in so many practical ways that he has tried, tested and proven to work.

And that's what this book is all about. It reveals the full story, the uncensored truth about every aspect of internet marketing taking you on the journey to success and busting a lot of myths along the way.

If you take the concepts in this book seriously, you will never have to suffer from marketing myopia ever again. Your online business efforts will be more targeted, and your results will become more predictable and measurable.

I created my multi-million pound property portfolio through internet marketing and like you have read many other books and courses in the past about internet marketing "secrets" and techniques, but they only told you half the story. This book will tell you the full story, so that you can free yourself from the dictates of the gurus and finally take control of your own business. Read this book carefully and with heightened motivation, because success is waiting for you behind every page.

Dave Griffin (Business Growth Co-Pilot and Social Media Leader)

Introduction

So, you want to know the full story. You want to know everything about internet marketing and how it can propel your business to huge financial success. Or for you, it may be that you just want to stop wasting money and time in what appears at this point to be the black hole that is; The Internet. I get that. In fact more than most I get that. You see, I have experience on both sides of the camp. I wanted the internet to propel my business success and I wanted it because I needed to stop haemorrhaging cash into making my online fortune!

This book began years ago with an experience that I will never forget, and I will continue to tell in order to save others from the same path. It was an experience that many internet marketing writers have never been through. I believe that sets this book up to be very different. In researching for this book, I have seen plenty of people who have some very positive examples of how online marketing has transformed their business. I have read accounts of how Twitter has been used to generate big deals. So how come I meet so many people who consider the same tool a waste of time? And imagine if I was writing this book only 3 years previously, there was no Twitter! Just like when you read this in the future and notice your favourite application is not listed.

MY Experience

My personal experience, the story that I believe sets this book apart is set in the year 2000. I had been running Urban Media for 3 years. It was the millennium and we all assessed what we were doing. For my part, I was running a successful website design business. I had some great brands; Sainsbury's, DHL, Tui Thompson, Orange to name a few. My friends and family thought this was pretty cool for someone at the time aged just 27. Me, I felt differently. I wanted something else. I was building websites for others to go on and be successful. I wanted my own website business and it had to be big.

I designed the concept for uk-trucking.net. This was to be a portal (large information website). It held information on a very wide variety of topics needed by the UK road transport industry. For those who don't know, it is a huge industry and without it, we all grind to a halt. It was so popular; we had 5 million visitors using the site every month. As a result, our list of advertisers was like a Who's Who at the top of the industry. The website included all the major truck manufacturers, Tyre people, Fuel providers etc. Our information was being used by others all over the place, with credits to uk-trucking.net in magazines and even in Shell training manuals!

Despite all of this, I hadn't learned how to monetise the raw success of the site. I knew nothing of affiliate schemes, failed to understand the business numbers and ultimately lost everything I had. The site looked great. I had come from a graphic design background and was in a very 'nuts and bolts' industry. It was at the top of Google for a massive list of keywords. We even had Pay per Click adverts running to boost numbers.

We had big name advertisers paying good money on a regular basis, but ultimately it still lost money; lots of money!

Eventually, I made the decision to stop funding the venture (time or money) and the site currently sits as the day this all stopped in 2003.

Guess what? The site makes more profit now with simple Ad-words running than it ever did! We still get enquiries and in the style of never say never, who knows, it may even be revived one day. But if I can say that (never say never), why is it not being revived this day, why wait? The simple answer is that I now know what is needed to make a successful website. I know that I have too many other projects on, to put in the energy or resources to go through the 'dip' between launch and success. If you know what will be needed and you can't commit, move on; even if only for a while.

The experience captured in the previous paragraphs opened the door for me to help others in a way that I would never have been able to before uk-trucking.net. I have to say that it took me a few 'sore' years to realise what a life changing experience had taken place. The uk-trucking.net project didn't blemish my CV; it enriched it in a way that I could never have chosen to do in any other way. I have walked the walk, I have worn the t-shirt. When I see an internet marketing campaign not working, I feel the way I did in 2003. This has led me to understand the full story of internet marketing.

The Full Story

With an industry and toolset that is ever changing, how can I ever suggest that a book with a definitive publish date can include the full story? Surely, as new social media sites come out, new browsers with new built-in tools and much more to come than we have ever seen before; it is impossible. I disagree. In fact, I can give you the full story within this introduction. Just like the guy who tells you the end of the film as you are walking into the cinema, I am going to reveal the full story right away. The rest of the book is simply an expansion of these bullet points;

- Before you begin, know your business numbers. With them, you know how much you can afford to spend gaining a new profitable customer.
- Work out how much you are worth to the unit of 1 minute. If you are happy to spend that amount per minute on your web guy, do it (whatever it is). If not, don't.
- Your free-time is not free time.
- If you don't have something of value to a potential customer, the web can't sell anything that you couldn't in person.
- Know that you have an audience and know clearly who they are.
- Target them and them alone.
- Have all your ducks in a row before inviting anyone to your website.
- If you can't convert 1 in a 1,000, why will you convert 1 in 10,000?
- Great design, sales copy, Google, Social media etc. etc. are all a means to an end, not the end. Don't ever forget what your end is.

Profoundly enough, the last paragraph does contain everything you need to know. The rest of the book truly is detail. It is the information that will back this up. And yet, by the end, there will be those who wanted more of an exactly how do I.... type manual. This book is aimed at giving you firstly guiding principles; things that will not change even if Google can't be found and Facebook goes back to Harvard. Then, secondly, we will explore some of the techniques used today. If you find yourself trying to copy the procedure to the letter, stop! They are examples to get your creativity going. If there was a one size fits all and delivers guaranteed results, everyone would do this.

So, who is this book for? Managing directors will get a 'light bulb' moment when they read how similar internet marketing is to any area of their business. Marketing managers will start to see why they have either failed to generate a return on their online spend or struggled to report its use back to the management team. Internet marketers will see a whole new side to what they currently do. Some will choose to ignore it. After all, it is easier to avoid responsibility. Others, you I hope, will read this book and understand the full weight of responsibility you have to achieve online success for your client, but also, see the fantastic sense of achievement that can be gained when you get it right.

This book is not for the faint hearted, but it is definitely for those who are ready to make a difference. I really hope you not only enjoy it, but also, find it extremely enlightening. I look forward to hearing about your successes.

De-mystifying the terminology

My pet hate; why does everyone have to pretend to be clever and talk in three letter acronyms and jargon? So, rather than putting a glossary at the back and allowing you to spend the entire book pretending you know what something means, but not really learning because like the majority, you weren't quite sure, I have put the 'Jargon Buster' section right up-front. **Feel free to skip this section, but remember it is better to learn this stuff first**, rather than to make assumptions and lose out on the real learning later in the book.

Above the Fold

'Above the fold' originates in print design. It refers to information that is displayed in the upper half of a page on a newspaper or magazine. The term is used by some web designers to indicate the placement of important information near the top of a web page. This ensures that the information is visible on screen when the visitor enters the page without having to scroll down.

Opinions change as to whether a page should scroll. I would say that you should provide a visitor with sufficient incentive to scroll. How interesting is your 'above the fold' content?

AdSense

AdSense is an advertising system provided by Google that enables web site owners to easily display advertisements on their web site.

Once the website owner has signed up for an AdSense account they copy and paste some code into their web pages and advertisements appear each time a visitor comes to their web site. The site owner then earns money each time a visitor clicks on one of the advertisements.

Analytics

This term has come to mean website usage statistics because Google provide a free statistics package called Google Analytics.

Web site analytics can measure information such as the number of visits to a web site, which countries the visitors are from, which pages they look at and what percentage of your visitors revisit your web site.

Affiliates

Affiliates are people who send visitors to another person's website and gain revenue either by doing so or based on the referred person taking action on the other person's website. One of the most well known affiliate schemes is run by Amazon. Anyone can sign up for their affiliate scheme and sell books and other products from their web site. The site owner earns a commission and Amazon take care of everything else

Alt Tags

When you use graphics or photography on a web page you should include Alt Text for each of these pictures. Alt Text is contained in an Alt Tag and is text that describes the picture so that visually impaired people using screen readers can have a description of the picture read out to them. Using the Alt Tag is also known to have added Search Engine Optimisation benefits.

Android

Android is a free mobile phone operating system. Think of it as Linux (an operating system which it is based on) as opposed to Windows. It is owned by Google, so watch out!

API

An API is an Application Programming Interface, but what does that mean!

It is in its basic sense a set of rules so that web developers know what information a third party software provider expects in order to send information back and forth between your software and theirs.

An example would be if I wanted to show LinkedIn profile data on my website. I would read the LinkedIn API to find out where I could get the data and how it would arrive. Web developers need to know more detail, but I find it best to stay with the simplified explanation.

App

An 'App' has been used to describe a programme written for a 'Smartphone'. Apple Inc. use the term App, within their 'App Store' to refer to these programs written for their iPod, iPhone and iPad devices. Apps are built for a huge range of purposes from leisure to business etc.

App Store

The App Store is Apple Inc's marketplace for buying Apps made by a wide collection of App Developers. For an App to be in the App Store, it must pass rigorous quality checks by Apple Inc.

Article Marketing

This is where you write articles about your specialist subject, service or product and provide them free of charge for others to publish on their web sites, blogs and newsletters. The benefits of article marketing are that when you provide articles for others to use, they include a credit to you and a link back to your web site. This helps in raising the profile of you or your organisation and it brings some more visitors to your web site.

ASP (.net)

ASP is Microsoft's means of creating dynamic (database driven) web pages.

A dynamic page differs to a static web page. Since web browsers can only view HTML, a dynamic page contains instructions for the server/database to carry out before creating an HTML page 'on the fly' and sending it to the browser.

Avatar

There are 2 uses for the term Avatar.

- Used as an 'icon' of a person for example on social media websites
- Used to build a clear picture of your ideal customer

Back End

Web sites which use information stored in databases are usually referred to as having a "Front-End" and a "Back-End".

The front-end is the part that we the visitors to that site see. The back-end is the administration area where members of staff can make changes to the web site such as changing prices in a database of products or adding new products.

This type of site by its nature is 'Dynamic' and therefore uses typically ASP (.Net) or PHP programming. There are other languages, but these are the most common.

Backlink

Otherwise known as backward links, this term refers to web pages that link to one of your web pages. It is the opposite of you placing a link on your site that points to a page on somebody else's website.

Blog

A blog is an online journal. Blog's are websites designed in such a way that the blog owner posts regular information (news, article comments, hints and tips etc.). The purpose is to add value and interest. In doing so, you begin to collect 'followers' who read your updates and a relationship is formed.

Blogging (posting blogs) is usually carried out as part of a social media strategy.

Browser

A browser or web browser is a programme installed on a computer, games console or mobile phone which is used to access the internet.

Creators of web browsers try to ensure that their browser complies with the W3C (industry) standards, but all browsers implement the standards to varying degrees. Web designers have to take these differences into account when testing their web pages to ensure that all of the web site visitors will be able to use the web site.

Browser testing

When a web designer builds a web site they (should) ensure that the web site looks and behaves as expected in a variety of the most common web browsers. The aim of browser testing is to ensure that the visitor to the web site will be able to use the site as expected and if certain visual features are not available, that this does not make the site unusable.

You would think that there was one standard that all site builders and browser makers conform to. There is, but the problem is, all of the different browsers (Internet Explorer, Chrome, Safari and Firefox etc) read the same website code in different way

Brochure site (brochure ware)

A simple website that shows company information. It has no 'dynamic' features or e-commerce type capability.

Captcha

When we sign up for services online, or log in to secure pages we are often asked to provide a username and password. Software is written to bulk test the logins and therefore gain fraudulent entry. The Captcha device is the image that you have to decipher on some forms. They can be annoying, but they are helping to secure your data and stop spam!

Trivia time! CAPTCHA stands for Completely Automated Public Turing test to tell Computers and Humans Apart. Alan Turing (the T in CAPTCHA) was a pioneering British computer scientist as well as working at Bletchley Park helping to crack the Enigma code.

Cascading Style Sheet (CSS)

A CSS file (or Cascading Style Sheet) is a file that is used to keep the layout and formatting of web pages consistent. Using Cascading Style Sheets also keep the actual web pages 'cleaner' and more optimised for both speed of download and search engine optimisation.

Chrome (Google Chrome)

Google Chrome is a website browser developed by the search engine giant Google.

Cloud

'The cloud' is a very generic term used to mean 'on the internet'. This is different to 'on the web'. The internet refers to the network of computer devices and the web refers to the network of pages found on the internet. There is a slight, but significant difference. Cloud is most commonly used as a prefix for terms to indicate that they are carried out on the internet, not on an individual's computer. Cloud storage involves storing your files online whereas cloud software (now including such regular tools as Microsoft Office) refers to programmes that run through the internet.

CMS (Content Management System)

CMS is an acronym of Content Management System and is widely used to describe software that is put in place to enable people to update and manage their own websites.

A CMS works in one of two ways;

- Stores the content used on web pages in an online database which can then be added to and edited by members of the organisation as part of the publishing process.
- Edits the HTML files and saves them to their original location.

Different people in an organisation can often be assigned different levels of access to a CMS. E.g. some people could be given the ability of adding new pages whereas others may only be able to edit or approve changes to existing pages.

CMS systems are great for giving clients access to change lots of content in-house, but they also allow clients to 'mess up' their websites too. Use with caution!!

Cookie

A cookie is simply a small amount of text data that a website can save on to your computer. It can store basic information such a membership number. This is how so many websites are able to "remember" who you are when you go back. This means that you don't have to fill in all your details each time you want to do something on a site like make a purchase.

A website can only access the cookies that it has created. It cannot access cookies from another website. Many people seem to think that cookies are harmful to their computer. They are only text files and cannot do anything to damage your computer.

Contextual Advertising

Many web sites and blogs carry advertising. Advertising brokers such as Google's AdSense make it easy for anyone who runs a web site to add advertising to their web site without having to build individual relationships with advertisers.

The advertising is known as contextual because a small piece of code is placed on each page of the web site and whenever the page is shown, advertisements which are relevant to the content of the page are displayed. This is seemingly magical process is achieved by the advertising broker using software to analyse the subject matter of a page and match up a relevant advertisement.

Database Driven

This term refers to websites that use a database to control the information seen on a website. Websites built in this way are also called 'Dynamic'. The page layout and the actual information are stored separately and then created 'on the fly' when you access the page. A good example would be a 'news' page or gallery.

DDA (Disability Discrimination Act) compliance

The DDA 1995 Act was written to ensure disabled users of services (including websites) had equal access to those services. On a website, this mainly affects the visually impaired. A website owner (not the developer) has the responsibility to ensure their site complies. The law covers how certain items are created, such as tables of data or use of font size and colour options.

Direct Traffic

When a visitor to a web site types the name of a web site directly into the address bar of their browser, they arrive at the site they have requested. This is called Direct Traffic. Web sites of well known companies with strong brands usually receive more direct traffic than other web sites.

Div Tags (div's)

The term 'div tag' refers to a way of laying out elements of a web page. Unless you are developing the website, you should not have to come across the term. However, it is used so freely by web developers that I felt it worth including!

Domain Name

The address of a web site is known as a domain name. Anyone can register a domain name if it is available. When you register a domain name, you do not own it, you are paying for the right to use it for a specific period. Most people register a domain for one or two years at a time, though they can be registered for up to 10 years at a time.

Dynamic

When a web page is referred to as 'dynamic', it simply means that the information displayed on the page has been stored separately to the visual layout of the page. This allows the website owner (or visitor in the case of User Generated Content) to update the information using a 'back end' system.

E-commerce

E-commerce websites are easily recognised by their ability to allow a visitor to locate and buy goods or services. They are 'online' shops. Since the transaction takes place on the website, they are sometimes called 'transactional' websites.

Electronic Commerce Regulations (EC Directive) 2002

The EC Directive was introduced to regulate online sales and how sellers sold goods/services to buyers using electronic means. The full regulations are found at;

http://www.legislation.gov.uk/uksi/2002/2013/contents/made

Entry Page

The entry page is the first web page that a visitor arrives at when visiting a web site.

It is often wrongly assumed that the most common entry page of every web site must be the home page. With so many visits coming through search engines, there is a very strong chance the entry page will not be the home page. In fact, it is not uncommon for 80-90% of web site traffic to come in at an entry page other than the home page.

Favicon

Favicons are small icons that appear in the address bar of a web browser and are specific to a particular web site. The term is short for Favourites Icon. Not all web sites have a favicon. You can tell those that do by the distinct icon in the mentioned address bar. When users save your web site (as a bookmark or in their favourites), the icon acts as a visual identifier for your web site.

Firefox

Firefox is the name of a web browser created by the Mozilla Foundation. This browser has a huge following and at the time of writing is second only to Internet Explorer in terms of number of users.

Flash

Flash was first introduced as a simple way to generate 'vector based' moving images on a web page. The initial benefit was file size. Since then, many very interactive website interfaces have been developed using the technology. Flash is also very popular as a video format and is the basis for YouTube videos. It is best used within a website rather than for the whole website.

FTP

File Transfer Protocol (FTP) is simply a method used to transfer files (web pages and associated graphics etc) from the 'local' computer that they have been created/edited on, to the web server (also known as the remote server). You may be asked for 'ftp details'. This simply means 'where' the server is (its address) and the username and password used to secure the server from unwanted access. The details are provided by your hosting provider.

Google

Google is such a big part of the internet experience that it barely needs introduction. It is the predominant search engine used for up to 90% of all searches carried out. Google has furthered its position by acquiring YouTube and creating many tools for web developers and web users (Google Webmasters and Google Docs). They have their own 'free' email (Gmail) and more.

Google Toolbar

The Google toolbar sits at the top of the browser 'window'. It contains useful features such as a search bar to save users from having to access the Google search page before carrying out a search. Internet marketers can also use the toolbar to gain knowledge of the pages that they are researching. This information could be 'Page Rank' or 'Backward Link' related.

Heat Map

A heat map is a picture of a web page that shows where users click when they visit a particular page. The areas that are clicked most often appear in red (hot spot), while the areas clicked least often appear in blue or with no colour at all.

Heat maps are a tool used by web developers as part of their website usability testing routines. This research could prove invaluable; however it is often avoided due to cost. There are other ways to view where people click on your site, but remember, understanding how your visitors behave when they visit your web site is crucial to improving its effectiveness.

A variant on the heat map based on mouse clicks, is an eye tracking heat map which gives an indication of what catches most people's eye when they visit pages on your website. You will require special third party software or an third party service if you wish to create a heat map of pages on your web site as they are currently not a standard part of analysis and statistics packages for tracking web sites.

Hits

A Hit on a website refers to a file being downloaded. It is often mistakenly used to refer to how many people have viewed the website. The reason this is inaccurate can be seen if a page is viewed by one person, once, but the page has 4 images on it. This would result in 5 hits; the page itself and the four image files.

Hosting Provider

The hosting provider is the person (usually business) that provides space and access to the space where your website is stored. This is typically connected with the provision of your email. This means the same provider is likely to deal with your email and web 'hosting'.

Http / Https

Quite simply, http is a 'protocol' used to send information over the internet from a web server, to your computer's browser. Https lets you know that the information has come to you and will be sent from you securely. This is used for data sensitive actions such as ecommerce checkouts. The 's' part does slow down the action and should only be used when the data needs to be transmitted 'safely'.

Internet Explorer

Internet Explorer is the web browser supplied by Microsoft with its Windows operating system. It is available for Mac, but Safari on Mac has become more popular especially through its inclusion within the Mac operating system and other portable Apple devices such as iPhone, iPod Touch and iPad.

iPhone, iPod, iPad

People are now accessing websites from a variety of devices. Currently, a very popular 'collection' is the 'i' range from Apple Inc. this has an effect on how a website should work; taking into account that the user will have a smaller screen, slower access and typically be mobile whilst accessing the site.

ISP (Internet Service Provider)

Your internet service provider is the person (usually Business) who provides you with access to the internet. Once you have a 'connection' to the internet, you are able to access websites and email. Whilst some ISP's do offer hosting and lots offer email, it is uncommon in business scenarios to get these services from an ISP.

JavaScript

JavaScript is a programming language which is most often used to add enhanced functionality to web pages. For example, JavaScript can be used to validate web forms, open new windows and allow for images to change when the cursor hovers over them. JavaScript runs locally (as opposed to remotely) and therefore is very reactive to the end user.

Joomla

Joomla is a completely free and open source Content Management System (CMS). It allows individuals and businesses to quickly and easily create a website. Within the Joomla community, there are many third party developers who contribute to the enhancement of Joomla via the development of various website extensions. It can be a cost effective web solution, however like the associated rigidity found with the majority of CMS systems, you may become restricted in what you can and can't do.

Keyphrase (keyword term)

Whilst many website owners focus on key words, we tend to search using terms or phrases. Setting pages up for key phrases is therefore a more productive way of gaining visitors through search engines. Imagine you want a Jaguar car. You are unlikely to simply type 'Jaguar' into your search engine.

You are more likely to search for 'Jaguar' 'Dealer' 'YourTown'. These three keywords make up your key phrase. A website should optimise its pages for key phrases that are likely to be used by the search engine user.

Keyword(s)

The list of words that your potential visitors are likely to use. In the example given under 'key phrases' previously, we have three keywords that are used to construct the phrase. All of these key words must be present to gain high search engine positions.

Keyword Density

This refers to the number of times a word appears in the text of your page in relation to other words. For example if you sell coffee machines and wish to be found in search engines under the term "espresso machine" you need to make sure that you espresso machine pages use this term frequently to ensure a high keyword density.

However, beware of overdoing it. Write naturally or the search engines may think you are artificially trying to manipulate your position in their index.

Landing Page

This is a marketing term used to describe a page on a web site that is designed specifically for a marketing campaign. It is often called a lead capture page. Visitors usually arrive at this page through online or offline advertising and the landing page will probably contain a special offer.

Various pages can be created for an advertising campaign to measure its effectiveness. Different variations of the landing page are sometimes tested to see which converts the highest number of visitors to customers.

Like

In Online Marketing terms, 'like' refers to a button placed on a page where a user can 'like' your content by clicking the button. This action results in the user's 'friends' seeing a link back to your website. I believe this 'like' function will begin to form the next level of link strategy as it is a more accurate indication to a search engine that your content is genuinely of value.

Merchant Account

A Merchant account is required for you to take payments online. This merchant account is used with a 'payment gateway' to collect card details securely from your customer and pass the funds into your account.

Mock ups (visual layouts and/or wireframes)

Part of the web design process is to present clients with a representation of what their web site will look like when finished. This enables the designer to obtain sign off on that stage of the project and to create discussion about any changes that may be required.

There are 2 elements. A wireframe simply shows where content may appear on the page. This is less often used unless the project is sizeable. The more helpful part to the customer is to see what the site will look like in colour. This is the 'visuals' part of a mock up. At this point the image is not a web page. It is presented to get the design sign off.

Organic Search

The term Organic Search means the non paid listings within a search engine. The model for a search engine is that they provide good quality listings of the information you have requested.

To appear at the top of the organic search results, you simply 'engineer' your pages to better suit the search engine 'algorithm', than all the other pages that compete to do the same.

Page rank

A significant part of the way Google (and indeed other search engines) rank a website is based on 'off the page' factors. These are built into a number referred to as Page Rank. Page Rank itself is used to cast a vote to another web page when a page links to another. For example, if a high 'Page Rank' page links to your page, it is helping your natural search listings.

Payment Gateway

A payment gateway is an online service that authorises credit and debit card payments for your web site. The payment gateway provides secure processing of your customers card details and then deposit the funds into your merchant account.

An internet merchant account and payment gateway are often set up in one process through the same company such as World Pay. It is important to note that if you are not using a 'third party payment processor' then you will need both a payment gateway and a merchant account.

PayPal

PayPal is probably the largest Third Part Payment Processor. They take care of payments from users and add the funds to you PayPal account.

From there, you can spend directly with other sellers that use PayPal, or transfer the funds to your bank account. With PayPal, you do not need a merchant account or payment gateway.

PHP

PHP is a programming language used to produce 'dynamic' web pages. It is the equivalent of Microsoft's ASP (.Net).

Podcasts

Podcasts are typically audio files created to be loaded onto mobile devices such as mp3 players for listening to at a later date. Quite often however, a user may stream the podcast over the internet and listen through their computer.

The content ranges from radio shows, to music mixes or even business communications.

PPC (Pay per Click)

Pay per Click is the term given to online advertising where you only pay for the 'clicks' you receive. This means that unless someone clicks on your advert and visits your website, you will not pay. Pay per Click systems (Google Adwords is the biggest) allow you to set lots of parameters such as maximum budget for the month, maximum for any 1 click, time of day etc. all adverts are shown for the keywords you select.

Protocol

When you hear the word protocol, it just means the 'rules' behind the message. It means one program can understand another.

Referring Site

Website 'traffic' is identified by where the visitor was before they arrived at your web site. When a person clicks on a link on a web site and arrives at another web site this is called a referral.

The site that the person clicks through from is called the referring site. Web analytics packages (such as Google Analytics) are used to analyse who is visiting your web site, can tell you where your visitors come from. This can be useful for tracking the success of promotions and advertising.

Safari

Safari is the web browser supplied by Apple with its Mac operating system. It is available for windows, but has become more popular through its inclusion within the other portable Apple devices such as iPhone, iPod Touch and iPad.

SERPs

When you use a search engine such as Google, Bing or Yahoo and enter a search term, the results that are returned to you are displayed on the Search Engine Results Pages (SERPs).

This term is mainly used by search engine optimisation specialists and you may never encounter it again. The main thing to know is that a successful optimisation campaign will see you on the top of the SERP's.

Screen Reader

A screen reader (often referred to as a 'text to speech' device) is a piece of software which interprets what is currently on a user's computer screen. The screen reader reads aloud what it finds on screen or outputs what it finds to a Braille device. Screen readers are used by the visually impaired.

It is important that web sites are built in such as way as to be accessible to screen readers and their users. There is even legislation (Disability Discrimination Act) that covers the correct construction of a website in this manner.

Screen Resolution

Unlike paper, screens vary in resolution and this has a huge impact on what a user sees when they look at your website. Imagine you write in your 'A4' notebook, but then you can only view that notebook half the width of 'A4'. You would have to scroll the page left to right. This is how it is with web pages.

Web designers have to make a 'best guess' as to the resolution your customers will use and deliver the best results to them whilst not causing too many difficulties to those on smaller or larger screen resolutions.

The introduction of a variety of devices leads to the requirement of different resolution sites for different devices.

SEO (Search Engine Optimisation)

Search Engine Optimisation simply refers to the process of matching the mathematical make up of your web pages to the requirements of the search engines. It is important that pages are not over engineered in favour of gaining positions rather than converting the visitors that you receive.

Server

The internet is built on a network of servers. You will hear them referred to as web servers or mail servers. They are very similar to a server in an office. The main difference is that they are connected to extremely fast internet connections, in secure buildings with things such as uninterrupted power supplies and fire suppressing equipment and temperature control.

Smart Phone

The way we access the internet and email has changed. Once, we used computers, now we use phones more than computers. This is across the board; it might not reflect your experience! This does affect how we view websites and therefore how we should display content to our prospective visitors.

Social Media

Social Media is a large subject area, but in its basic form refers to various websites that accept user generated content. This allows you to promote yourself/business through them. There is certain etiquette to using these sites and users that overly advertise their wares are frowned upon. The basic principle is to get involved in the community and provide value to the particular community. The list of social media sites grows, but we have included a section on the current top social media sites later in the book.

Silverlight

Silverlight is Microsoft's powerful development platform for creating rich media applications. It is an equivalent of Flash, but uses the Microsoft .Net 'framework'.

Sitemap

A sitemap is a page where all of the links of a website are laid out. They are typically shown in the hierarchy that they exist on your website.

SSL

This refers to a 'secure' server. You will see 'https' in the address of pages stored on a secure server. You may also see the 'padlock' icon.

Static Web Page

In a static web page, the creator of the page uses HTML to build it, and then uploads it to the server. When someone visits the page, the same content that the designer created is downloaded to the visitor's computer and displayed in their web browser.

SQL (SQL Server)

SQL (pronounced Sequel), is a database language. SQL Server refers to any database that implements the Structured Query Language. You may hear the term when referring to Microsoft's MS SQL (e.g. SQL Server 2008) or MySQL (the free, typically PHP backed SQL database). What you should know is that SQL databases are better than say Access database for building scalable websites as they are typically 'multi-threaded' meaning more than one person can be in the database at one time.

Third Party Payment Processor

If you want to take credit card and other forms of payment online and you do not have a merchant account, you can use a **third-party payment processor**. These companies let you use their process payments via their merchant account and then transfer the money to your own bank account. This is quicker and often less expensive and certainly less 'hassle' than gaining your own merchant account. However, for larger transactional sites, this option may prove inadequate.

The best known third-party payment processor is PayPal.

Thumbnail

A thumbnail is a reduced version of an image which can be clicked on to show a larger version of the image.

This is commonly seen in online shopping web sites where a small photograph of a product is shown on the product information page and the visitor has the option to inspect a larger, more detailed picture. They do this by clicking the 'thumbnail'. It is also common to see online picture galleries laid out as thumbnail photographs, each of which can be clicked to reveal the full size photograph.

Transactional

Used when referring to a transactional website. These sites take care of the entire sales process and are also known as e-commerce sites. The term comes from the fact that the sale is 'transacted' on the website.

User Generated Content

Any text, images, video or audio which is added to a web site by one of the web sites visitors is considered to be **User Generated Content (UGC).**

Websites are becoming increasingly interactive and therefore contain a wide variety of user generated content. This model provides benefits to the website owner including;

- Providing content at little or no expense to the web site owner
- Adding a degree of credibility to the opinions on a web site e.g. book or restaurant reviews
- increasing interactivity between the web site and its readership

On the down side, it can require a lot of monitoring in order to ensure that the web site is not abused.

Later in this book, we will look at Social Media. All social media sites are perfect examples of User Generated Content.

User

A user is a commonly used term for someone who uses your web site or your software. Users could also be referred to as visitors in relation to your website. All elements of the website should be built with the 'user' in mind.

Visitors

Many people talk about "hits" when measuring how busy their website is, but 'hits' refers to how many files have been requested from the server to make up all of the pages that have been viewed. 'Visitors' is a much more useful measurement as it refers to how many people visited a web page/site.

You will see the terms 'visitors' and 'unique visitors' used. Whilst visitors refers to every new visit the web page receives regardless of whether the person has visited the site before, the term unique visitors, as the title suggests, counts each new visitor whereas a repeat visit would not be counted.

The difference means different things to different sites. A membership site would expect and want a lot of repeat visits. A business that used their website to attract new visits who then deal via email rather than needing to go back to the website, should be looking for a lower 'repeat' visits and therefore a higher unique visitor percentage.

Visibility

This is a very general term used by web designers and web marketers to refer to how easy your web site is to find using a search engine. How 'visible' is it?

More specifically, you would look at your visibility in relation to the specific search terms (key phrases) that will help bring people to your web site.

W3C (World Wide Web Consortium)

The World Wide Web Consortium works on web standards. I describe these standards as being like iso9001 for the internet. When you hear terms such as HTML5, this is a standard; a set of rules that web developers and browser providers should adhere to. You should check that your pages are W3C compliant. This is the best a developer can do for you.

Web Stats

'Web stats' is a now old term for analytics. It refers to the statistics that website statistics/analytics tools can give you. This information should be used to continually 'tweak' a website to constantly improve its effectiveness.

White Space

White space is a page layout term and refers to the areas of a web page that have no text or graphics on them. White Space has been used as a term for many years before the web existed. Although not always 'white', it is the space that allows everything else to be read clearly.

When (in print or online) there is too much information and everything is cluttered. This is a lack of white space.

XML Sitemap

An XML sitemap is the equivalent of that a sitemap but this type is provided to search engines in a format they can read and then use to 'index' a website's pages correctly.

Before we begin

I firmly believe that the majority of internet marketing projects would be so much more successful if the people running them would take the effort to plan and set targets before doing anything else. We all have a tendency to just dive into things, but how often do we have to stop and look at things afresh. Look at things that we should have put in place at the start. How often do you hear the term 'hindsight'? Now, I agree that planning cannot solve everything and sometimes we have to just DO things and stop talking about them. Indeed, you can plan to death and layout certainties that are in fact projections and not certain at all. The point of planning is so that we get as close as we can, to knowing what outcomes we can expect, before we waste valuable resources of time and cash.

This section is about just that. Planning it all out and knowing what outcomes you need to achieve. Finding out the key numbers so that any measuring we discuss in later chapters has relevance. Without this, statistics are simply numbers of no significance.

Before we get into this, there is something even more crucial. I regularly sit in meetings where professionals and clients alike use terms that sound BIG. The problem is; the client doesn't want to appear stupid so they go along with it. They have been spoken to in a foreign language and just accepted it. After all, this is far better than looking stupid right?? WRONG! There is an amazing power behind looking stupid when it's appropriate. You see, it is the 'techie talking' guy that is truly stupid. They believe that using all those three letter acronyms makes them sound clever. Now that is truly stupid.

I used the first chapter deliberately to de-mystify some of the terminology. If you are still not sure about some of the techno terms and skipped the chapter, please go back! The rest of the book will be of a lot more value.

In this chapter we will look at various parts of the planning stage. We will also look at various options and show that sometimes we get caught in a box. We all try to think outside the box, but then sometimes we just go right ahead and think inside it anyway.

Plan, Plan and Plan

It's an old cliché that if you fail to plan, you plan to fail. Whilst I don't want to focus on the negative aspects of what no planning means, it is very true. Online marketing is no different to any other part of your business. In fact it is becoming increasingly important to get this particular piece of your business jigsaw right.

Planning, by my definition, is to do a full dry run before committing to anything. Planning will involve a storyboard of what your website visitor will experience when they encounter you online. It will include every possible step that they may take and every 'diversion' that you will use to get your potential customer to the right place before their attention span has been exceeded.

Your potential site visitor may find you in a variety of ways. Depending on your online marketing mix (discussed later), they may have seen you on YouTube, read about you on a blog, followed your various tweeting or simply done a search for someone that offers what you do and you came up top! But that is just the beginning. What happens then? One thing we can be sure of is when they click onto your site, there is far more chance that they will land on a page other than your home page, than on the home page itself. This means you have many possible entry points or as we (web guys) call them; Landing Pages. From any one of these Landing Pages, what can your prospect see, why should they stay, where could they go next and number one on the list; what is your desired outcome?

Your Avatar

Before we can start to work that out, we need to know who they are likely to be. We call this your Avatar. You need to know who your perfect customer is. Once you can define this, you can start to build your website around them. A lot of marketers fail to understand the concept behind this approach, and a lot of business owners can't get to grips with focusing on just one customer. Allow me to explain! I am not suggesting that you only have one stereotype of a customer. However, what I do believe is that when you try to build a web page to suit everyone, it inevitably fails to suit anyone.

Creating an avatar is easier than you might think. First, get a list of your existing best customers (or if you are a new business, who you would like to work with). Who do you need to attract within those companies? If you want micro businesses, then you will be dealing with the owner. In larger companies it may be the marketing person or procurement or accounts? Work out who you deal with and list them. Now, what do they have in common? Are they all of a certain age group? Are they in the same income band? What else do they buy? Look for common themes and then build an imaginary prospect that is just like your existing best customers. You can even repeat this for your worst customers! Whatever you do on your web pages (or any marketing) target your ideal avatar without trying to appeal to everyone. Where you can, you should intertwine a message that would actively put off your avatar of a 'bad' customer. Not all business is good business!

So, how do you speak directly to your best customer avatar and intertwine a message that puts off your bad customer avatar? This too is simple. You will see that the lists you have created of each are a list of opposites. Where one will be price conscious, the other will appreciate quality more etc. if your target prospect places a higher priority on quality than price, speak of this in your web page text. If speed is an issue, highlight your quick turnaround. Just remember, Quick Turnaround, Attention to Detail and Lowest Price are three requirements. One has to have priority. You should not try to be all things to all people.

Your specific Niche

Another area you need to consider and will have a big effect on your avatar is your niche. Look at all of the brands you aspire to; they have a niche or at least built their name on a niche. A niche is quite simply your specific offering. Urban Media help companies to get return on investment through new media technology. We do not focus on Design, we do not focus on Social Media or any other area, we carry out these tasks, but our niche is Return on Investment. It is clear in all we say. When you have a niche, pin your colours to it. Do not be frightened of putting others off. Your niche (and avatar) is your passport to success. We are very clear that if someone puts the visual design of their web page higher than getting a return on their investment, they are not an ideal partnership for us.

When you find a niche, you can 'own' it. You are the specialist. You are the one to come to when I need someone to do what it is your niche covers. Since you are the specialist and since you are the one person I need to talk to, I am willing to pay more. Why? Because I value getting things done right, first time! It makes financial sense.

If you attract customers that are not 'in sync' with your culture and whether you know it or not, you have one, you are setting yourself up for failing. Knowing your niche, promoting your niche and sticking to your niche, all help to avoid an easy pitfall. When your customer has the same values as you, they are on the same hymn sheet. They naturally 'get' what it is you do for them and they find it easy to refer you to others. When you sell out to a customer who does not share your values (usually through fear of losing the customer) it is easy for you to spend more time trying to convince the customer of what you are

Middle Aged Mum found wearing Abercrombie and Fitch!

Abercrombie and Fitch know who their target customer is. They have even been in trouble for knowing who their target employee is!

They target the well-off youngster. Their fashion is at odds with their Savile Row address, but all of this is deliberate. As you walk through the doors of their London Home, you are greeted by a model wearing jeans and a six pack! The music is loud and the lighting is dim. There are dancers on the balcony and every member of staff carries the model look. This is youth culture and it is unashamed.

Now, watch people walking around London and further afield. The majority of people wearing Abercrombie and Fitch are indeed the youth culture that fits the 'A&F' Avatar. However, you will see a healthy collection of Middle Aged Mums (and dads) carrying the famous Moose logo.

doing for them than you actually spend doing the task. If you have to convince customers of your value, you have a mismatch that is draining you and affecting other 'in sync' customers. Find your niche, work out your avatar and be specific when you 'recruit' customers.

There are lots of resources around finding and owning a niche, this book is not designed to explore the full details of finding and owning your avatar or niche. It is however, crucial that you do work this out. As we go through this book, you will get lots of information on how to create a winning internet marketing campaign. Remember though, if you are not clear what you want, then what you get will not be clear either! Internet marketing has the power to transform your business in positive ways, but beware, time skipped here, will show in heaps later.

Start with the end in mind

Now you have a clear vision of your avatar and in which niche you operate in, you can begin to work out your desired outcomes. To do this, we work back to front. The only way to streamline the process of receiving a visitor and converting them into a customer is to start with the end in mind. There is a full chapter on converting website visitors into customers later. For this chapter, you just need to get really clear as to what you want your internet marketing to achieve. Will you sell online; are you filling a seminar? Do you simply want to build an email list? What do you want to do with the list? How are you going to monetise the website? How do you get the maximum return on investment?

This part should tie in with your wider marketing and business plan. You should answer questions like who will pick up the enquiries. Can you cope with the increase in business? How much investment do you have to put into this venture? What return are you expecting?

Next we will discuss your key numbers. This will help you to understand how to convert the financial targets you have into actions that need to take place on your website. As you grow your internet marketing, it will be imperative that you measure outcomes. They will be easier measured in non financial numbers. Since we are focused on Return On Investment, this will need to relate to financial success. For this reason, you should carry out the exercises on the 'know your numbers' section as they will make up a large part of your planning. Knowing how many 'conversions' is important. Without this, you will not know whether you are on target, dangerously low, in need of further resource etc.

Starting with the end in mind means sorting out all of the detail in terms of being very clear about what you want to achieve, how you will achieve it and what it will mean to the rest of the business. There are no guarantees, but being clear is a way to have direction. Without clarity and direction, you are at the mercy of every other external factor. Even if you do not achieve all of the goals you set out in your initial planning, by going through the process, you will be a lot closer than if you had not planned at all. The great news is that because this is the part that others avoid, you will be leagues ahead of your competitors from the beginning.

Know Your Numbers

Failing to understand the key numbers that drive your business could be limiting your growth and financial success. These numbers are relevant both online and offline. The great thing about online marketing is everything is very measureable. This makes it even more worthwhile knowing what numbers you need to systemise your online success.

Lifetime Customer Value (LCV)

Often we fail to realise that the value of a customer is in the lifetime of the relationship. This can cause us to make cutbacks in recruiting customers as we do not see the real key number. Big companies realise this and use this in everything they do. They admittedly can afford to cash flow things easier and we will discuss this in the next section.

To work out your Lifetime Customer Value, first divide your total sales revenue over a period (a Year is best) by the number of customers that brought that revenue. This provides you with your Average customer spend for that period. Once you have this, multiply it by your gross profit margin. The result is your average customer profit for that same period. Remember, it is important to calculate this using your gross profit margin. Without taking away the cost of any sales, you could be generating new customers unprofitably.

Finally, how long do you keep customers for? You need to work out how many 'periods' you keep customers for (again, the average) and multiply this by your average customer profit for the period. This is then, how much profit an average customer brings you each [year] and how many [years] you will keep them. This equation covers all possibilities. It may be that your customers spend once but in a large way (double glazing) or they may have regular small

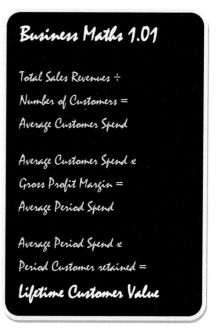

Business Maths 1.01

Total Sales Revenues ÷
Number of Customers =
Average Customer Spend

Average Customer Spend x
Gross Profit Margin =
Average Period Spend

Average Period Spend x
Period Customer retained =
Lifetime Customer Value

amounts (subscription services) or more typical, a mix of the former. This is your lifetime customer value.

Having calculated your lifetime customer value, you can begin to see at which point your customer acquisition becomes unprofitable.

The Compound Effect

There is one other element. I tend to leave this out of the equation and use it as a bonus! For every customer you get, how many referrals do you receive? Imagine I pay £1,000 to acquire a new customer. Their lifetime customer value is £1,200. I am on the right side of profitable, but only just. However, when I consider that the happy customer refers me to 1 new customer per year over the life of our 5 year relationship, the 'actual' lifetime customer value grows. You could suggest by 5x £1,200. This is a start, but of course, the new customer they referred you to is also happy. They go on to also refer you to 5 other people and so on, and so on. One of the main ways we promote the use of new media is to work harder for your existing customers. This last paragraph, especially if you had not considered the compound effect before, should have just turned your internet marketing plans on their head! The only issue to look at is your customers spend profile.

It is easy for many businesses to see how they could make a massive return on their investment once they look at the Lifetime Customer Value model and especially with the Compound Effect. The challenge is as always whether you can cash flow the exercise. I speak of return on Investment, but without the investment, there is no return. The higher the investment, often yet not always, the bigger the return will be. However, you need to know just how much you can invest. If your customers make their major purchase at the point of first sale, this will make a huge difference to if your customer signs up to a long term, low monthly subscription. It may be that the second profile is far more profitable over the long term, but it is harder to cash flow in the early days.

Cost of Acquisition

The final piece of the jigsaw in terms of knowing your numbers is the price you pay for a new customer. This is another simple number to generate. Take your total sales and marketing activity over a period of time and divide that number by the number of customers that came as a result. Remember, the period that you 'gained' the customer may differ slightly to the period that you made the investment. When you work this out you should consider your own time too. Remember, every minute you spend on one thing is a minute you can't spend on another. What are you worth? What is one minute of your time worth? Measure it or you will set yourself up to become a busy fool. I see it! People editing their own websites, spending hours on Social Media and working late?

Once you know how profitable a customer is to you over the long term, you can use your cost of acquisition to evaluate whether you should start, continue or stop any marketing activity. This approach should be used to assess your online marketing too. If Pay per Click works for you, use it; if writing a blog doesn't, don't. If the effort and cost to gain and keep a first page listing in Google, for the key term you need, is not worth the reward, don't just do it 'because' you feel you should.

You have to be really practical with this area. If you have got this far in, you are clearly more serious about your online success than many. When I wrote this, I anticipated that just as when I speak at various events, the majority would try to skip straight to the 'doing' chapters. They fail to see that the real key is in this chapter. I make no apologies, but I do commend you for sticking with it. When I was a boy, I learned to play the drums. I had seen the drummers with their drum kits and I wanted to be the same. I got a big shock when we spent months learning the rudiments (paradiddles, flams etc). When you watch your favourite band, you see the effects of a group of people who have gone over the details. You don't see the actual details. In the same way, getting the details sorted now will create big success later.

Think it Through

It sounds common sense, but sadly, common sense is not all that common, so at the risk of me stating the obvious, you really need to think everything through before committing to a particular route. The following sections are designed to help you think differently about your website.

Quite often, clients come to me and they know exactly what they need. They have looked at other websites and copied a list of the pages that they need and start to recite them. Home, About Us, Services, Contact and so on. The problem is; this is simply a list of what someone else has decided to use. They have no evidence that the combination works, just an assumption. With hindsight, this is probably not the best way to decide upon such a critical area of your business.

When is a website not a website?
I try to encourage all of my clients to start with a blank page. This can seem strange at first, and I would even say that often we end up with similar pages to the list they may have brought in. The difference is that by coming at the task from a different angle, the subtle differences make a far better website.

We have uncovered some amazing 'jewels' by asking lots of 'why' and 'who cares' questions. It may be that you have only recently begun looking at websites. You may not remember what websites were like in the 90's for example. We couldn't do half of what we can now. This didn't happen because everyone just copied the last person. This evolution of increased usefulness has come about by people willing to consider that a website doesn't have to be a website like every existing website.

For example, I remember when a '2 step' animated graphic (gif) saying 'under construction' was advanced! Now, we build websites that auto duplicate pages, create different outputs for the back office accounts or despatch departments and this isn't the end. There is a lot more to come. So the question is more likely to be "what do you want a website to do?", rather than "what does a website do"?

So, I encourage you to take a blank piece of paper once you have worked through this chapter and consider what you want your website to achieve. You can then start to work backwards with what that means you need to have in place. This is a far better way than starting with a list of pages that need populating.

To sell or not to sell

Why does everyone think they need to sell online? I am not saying you don't need to, but also importantly; I'm not saying you do. I believe you have to work this out based on the merits of what return you expect for what investment needs to go in. Setting up an e-commerce system is far more than simply buying an off the shelf ecommerce system or even having a bespoke (recommended) solution created.

Selling online often means changing your existing business model to include Mail Order functions. Is this what you thought you would be doing when you decided to sell online? You see, I have a view on this. Firstly, if you feel that you could just get your existing staff to send out a couple of parcels within their current role, then how do you see that returning you a significant amount for your investment? I suppose conversely you could say; if you expect to make a significant return, then how do you expect current staff to take up the strain. The net result of either under estimation is poor customer service and a huge knock on effect to long term profits.

I believe there are many opportunities for businesses to sell online. I also believe that if you are aware of the

Garden Centre web-shop plans not so concrete

A Local Garden centre was convinced they had to have an online shop. After all, everyone said so. To their surprise, I asked them why?

Whilst discussing the subject, it came out that it wasn't very practical to take stone ornaments to the post office in jiffy bags. We also found that the garden centre had food that should win awards in their cafeteria. And yet, the place was not as busy as they could cope with.

It was an obvious suggestion to use budget that would have gone into building an online shop to get people into the garden centre. These 'converts' would spread the word and generate more profit, quicker and without the attached (and often unseen) hassle of an ecommerce solution. Stage 2, who knows, maybe a book on Amazon, sharing the secret recipes!

full investment and can cash flow it, then online sales could be a great expansion plan for your business.

Do remember though Elton's law of flip?! If you are to start competing online, selling a commodity product, then you will be fighting on price. The internet is where we all go for a cheap bargain.

So what is the 'flip'? Well, you could enter this market and make additional profits, albeit less per product, for your business. The flip is that your existing customers will not want to pay a higher price in store than they do online. You need to consider what your online and offline pricing strategy is. This may mean altering the range for each medium. Maybe online sales are only for 'bulk' purchases? This is one for you to consider on a case by case basis.

EBay Shops and Amazon Seller

If you do decide to sell online and you are low on budget, do you need your own shop? Building, maintaining and promoting your own shop is expensive. There is no getting around this. The cheaper 'off-the-shelf' options are ok, but they have limitations. The credible suppliers of these systems would even agree. They are great to get you going, but not so great in the long run or if you need to do extensive search engine optimisation for example.

You could consider selling solely through EBay or Amazon. I tend to think of these 'marketplaces' as like taking a shop in a shopping centre rather than building your own on a farm out of town. If you built your own, you would get lots of control, the 'rent' may be less and you would not have to compete with anyone on your doorstep. All sounds good, but how would you get customers to your shop and away from the shopping centre? It may be better, especially in the beginning, to sell through these marketplaces. You will build up a customer base and potential customers WILL see your products from day one. You just focus on getting the right products out at the right prices. At the same time, give fantastic customer service. Both EBay and Amazon have systems built in where sellers are 'graded'.

There are many books around the subject of buying and selling through both EBay and Amazon. This section is not an exhaustive detail of 'how to do it' or 'what sells well'. You can refer to the growing collection of books for that. This section is here to suggest adding the use of EBay and/or Amazon to your thought process. Remember, whatever method you choose, if you do indeed choose to sell online; the goal is to make the most return on your investment.

DIY or hire a PRO

This is easy! Do you fix your own car? How about carry out your own dentistry? So why would you build your own website? Why would you carry out your own internet marketing?

Despite me making it that simple, you may be tempted to suggest to yourself that this is different. You can do your own website and get it to the top of Google. Well, I will agree with you. I know you can. My reasoning behind recommending that you do not do the work yourself is different. It is based 100% on profit; making you as profitable as possible.

If you are a web designer, then I am flattered that you are reading this, but it will not teach you any of the 'how to's...' that you don't already know. If you are not a web designer, I am guessing you have a 'day job'; a role within your business that someone relies on you to perform. I am a creative thinker and strategist. An odd combination I know, but that is what I do. It would not be profitable for me to 'optimise' my own websites. I pay people to do that. They are specialists. They know the very detail, even as it changes. In fact, I should thank them for their input into later chapters in this book. Team, thank you!

I calculate whether someone should do this work, based on their own value to their business. What is your hourly rate? What are you worth? If you are like the majority of UK businesses as I write this, you may want to think of this in terms of what you should be worth! The recent recession will pass and even with the many economic 'measures', you still have to build your business on the same principles. In fact, it is even more important that you use outsourcing at this time. It keeps overheads down. One thing for sure, you should be focused on the top level direction. Not the detail. Hire a Professional. Just like fixing your own car may seem like a money saving idea, we all know that it doesn't work in the long run.

Google & Social Media are not the answer!

If only I had a penny for every person who walks into our office and states they need to be number one in Google. Or maybe a penny for every business owner in networking circles who bestows the virtues of Social is convinced that their recent tweet about taking 'fluffy' the dog for a walk was part of their 70/30 mix of personal and business tweets!

Let me dispel a myth. Google is not the answer. While I am on the myth-busting train, here's another; Twitter is not the answer. I could go as far as saying that all of the single elements of a successful website and online marketing strategy are not the answer. You see, the secret is the recipe. Try making a cake without flour. It wouldn't taste much like cake. And yet, good cake is definitely worth eating right?

My point in this section is this. The secret to a successful web strategy is to know and continue to focus on the objectives. All of the elements are just that. Flour is just flour. Eggs are just eggs, sugar is sweet, but it is just sugar. Add them together in the right order and the right amount, and you get a successful outcome. Do not get tied up following a fad. Fads end. Business success (or failure) is constant. Online success is just a part of your business success. Do not pin its hopes on a fad.

Right now, a lot of people will be confused as to why I called Google a fad. Try talking to my grandma. She doesn't know what Google is. When I have grandchildren, will they? What is sure is that these mediums come and go. Use them to best advantage; just remember that the objective is a constant. The elements change.

PC, Mac or Smartphone?

The ever changing skyline means that now, you need to have a presence across various devices. It used to be that a website had to work in a variety of web browsers, across PC's and Mac's. Of course now, we view the internet just as often through a Smartphone. If you deliver the same website to a Smartphone user as you do your full screen web visitors, you will not create success. The big companies know this.

A journey round the Apple 'App Store' will reveal that not only do the major players invest heavily in being Smartphone ready, they produce specific 'Apps' to make sure their users on various platforms get the best experience. For small businesses, I suggest a more practical approach. It is possible to have a Smartphone specific website so that users of any Smartphone can view your pages in a specifically designed format. In fact, they don't even have to go to a different website address. It is possible too for your web developer to create a website that detects the type of device used to access the page and deliver the right content to that user at that specific time.

At one time bigger and bigger screens were the fashion. Currently, we are choosing more portable devices that in turn mean smaller screens. In years to come, the devices will have changed. What shouldn't change is your understanding that you need to be viewable on all variety of devices from games consoles to phones and even computers!

Building a tribe

What the internet does allow us to do is to build tribes easily. I was first introduced to tribes by Seth Godin. Seth is a writer, blogger, speaker etc. on the subject of marketing. He challenges the status quo. The theory of tribes though is not, in my view, radical. It is an obvious observation that we fail to see because it is too obvious. The wood for the trees springs to mind.

The theory is that we all belong to tribes. This may be our religious tribe, our coffee house tribe, our fashion tribe etc. we 'buy into' the tribe and spread the message of the tribe. The tribe leader speaks the message and the tribe disperse the message to their circle of influence, which disperse it to theirs etc.

What Seth argues, and I agree, is that the internet makes it easier to build niche tribes that connect with the audience. So, consider that not everyone in your local area is as committed as you to providing products and services that are high quality, ethically sourced. You would struggle to build a scalable business. The target audience would not sustain you. Your option is to add cheaper, not so ethically sourced offerings or restrict your business growth with potentially fatal results. Whereas online, you can fly your flag, whatever shape and colour that flag is. Online, there is a huge audience and we have the tools to connect. Online, all we have to do is be 'worth' following and people will want to amass around us.

It is therefore quite apt that this chapter which started with the words 'before we begin', ends with the real secret to success both online and offline. A prequel to this secret to success is that online is only another media. So the secret is this. Find out what you are really good at. Really good at; passionate about, excited about. Analyse who your perfect partner would be in your pursuit to provide this passion and knowledge to them. Remember, recruit customers, and don't just 'take them on'. Life is too short. Choose whom you want to work with based on their shared passion for what it is you supply and they need. Then deliver it consistently and profitably, based on knowing your key numbers. The rest will come.

The following chapters are all about the mechanics. You could miss a couple and still succeed. Miss out on finding out what you want and I would suggest it will be far easier to fail.

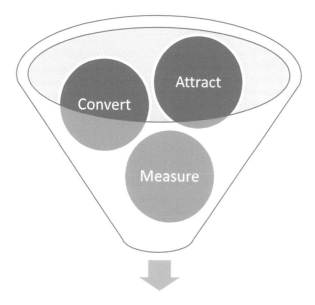

Online Success!

Add 'continued conversation'
for Online Success Nirvana!

Quick Recap

- ✓ If you fail to plan, you plan to fail
- ✓ Create an avatar of your best customer
- ✓ Create an avatar of your worst customer
- ✓ Not all business is good business
- ✓ Find your niche; specialists earn more
- ✓ Know what your 'desired outcome' is
- ✓ Start with the end in mind
- ✓ Do a full dry run on paper first
- ✓ Know your numbers
- ✓ Lifetime Customer Value
- ✓ Customer Spend Profile
- ✓ Cost of Customer Acquisition
- ✓ Remember the Compound Effect
- ✓ A website is a media, not a format, question it
- ✓ You don't have to sell online
- ✓ If you want to sell online, consider EBay and Amazon
- ✓ Call in the Professionals. You will save in the long run
- ✓ Do not skip the detail, it will cost in the long run
- ✓ Make sure your site views correctly on a variety of devices
- ✓ Build a Tribe by being 'good' and sticking to your niche

After each Chapter, we will have discussed a lot of idea changing topics. They will apply to you differently depending on your exact requirements in relation to budget, industry, approach and more. This page is for you to write any ideas that have come to you whilst reading the last chapter. If it is blank and you have nothing to add, re-read the chapter! This time, think of each section in relation to your business.

Attract

For those that have attended one of my 'Internet Marketing: The breakthrough seminar' events, the rest of the book will be in reverse order!

I have written the book in chronological order in terms of the prospect to customer process. That said I should throw a strong word of caution in at this point. If you currently receive 100 visitors and convert none, do not assume your problem is a lack of visitors. Simply attracting more visitors will not fix your problem. A zero percent conversion rate is a zero percent conversion rate. If you had 10,000 visitors, how many would you expect to turn into customers with your zero percent conversion rate?

Word of caution out of the way, let's get into looking at ways to attract more visitors (traffic) to your site. The key, is gaining relevant traffic. You need to attract visitors that will be genuinely interested in what you have to say or offer. Too often people are tempted to choose the high volume keyphrase because they still believe in the 'spam like' numbers game. They believe that all you need is a lot of people on your website and some will convert. Won't they? Please!

It seems ridiculous to me that they never stop to think of their own experiences. If I am looking for a Mercedes dealer and through some 'clever' keyphrase 'stuffing', the local BMW dealer came up in my search; I would not change my lifelong desire to buy a Mercedes. Yes, the BMW dealer had achieved a high listing for a term where they may pick up a lead from their competitor, but not only is this unlikely, it is energy spent in the wrong place.

As we begin to discuss Keyphrase research and Competitor Analysis, remember at all times that relevance is the key. It is far better to attract 100 relevant visitors than 10,000 non relevant drifters. The end goal (and only one we are ultimately interested in) is converting people from 'searchers' to 'customers'.

Keyphrase research

Keyphrase (or keyword) research is one of the starting points for any type of online marketing. For an online marketing campaign to be effective it is essential that the company is aware of which key phrases they need to target.

In order to identify these necessary key phrases, a wide range of research must take place and be analysed. To some, they will simply take a 'stab in the dark' and aim for the words and phrases that they assume others will use. If there is one practise that should be banned in this area, it is assumption. There are a lot of tools to help you to make a far more educated decision in relation to keyphrase research.

The first thing you need to do is to brainstorm as many phrases as you feel are relevant to your business. Think big and throw your net wide. You will be getting rid of a lot of the terms, but first, get them all out. Break down everything that you do. Come up with a long list for each subject. Build in plurals, combinations and even use the thesaurus.

Once you have your lists, think about what your ideal customer (Your Avatar) would look for. Speak to them. Get them involved. Ask "if you were looking for a company that did what we do for you, what would you search for?" you will see at this point that the list is growing and possibly shrinking at the same time. They will have different ideas to yours. It is they however, that are better placed to answer the question. Remember, you are trying to attract more of them, not more of you!

The third method that should be used is to look at your competitor websites. What terms do they use? To find this out, look at the 'title' bar at the top of the browser when you view their webpage. You could even 'view source' by using the right mouse (on PC) options. Look through the code and although you may not understand it all, you will see repeated words or words near the term 'meta' (title, description, keywords). Look specifically for anything useful in between <H1> and </H1>. These are tags used by developers to let search engines know what the search engine should give weight to on a page.

Once you have this long list, you can enter the terms into a 'keyword suggestion tool'. This is something for your internet marketers, so rather than going into details of which ones to use etc. I will keep the paragraph to the point that these tools will add even more ideas to the pot, but they will also help you to define which words to go for. Your strategy should be to review the full list of words and the levels of both 'traffic' and 'competition'. Internet marketers also look for the strength, not simply number of competition.

The pattern to look for will be;

- At the top, you will see phrases with lots of searches performed on the phrase every day. These will have huge competition. Avoid them for the short term. You will spend too much time TRYING to get on the first page and will not get there in the near future!
- At the bottom, you will see words with very little competition that you could easily get on the first page of all the search

engines, but it would do you little good due to the low level of searches performed on the phrase.

- In the middle, there will be terms that have sufficient searches carried out and also low enough competition to allow your pages to gain high enough listings within a decent timeframe. These are the ones you want.

When I point this out to clients, occasionally, a client is adamant that they want the big hitting key phrases. Let me explain; it is not impossible to get any keyphrase to the top of any search engine. The process as we will see is one of mathematically engineering your pages to be better than all the others. This is not difficult. It is however, often time consuming. You will be paying for either your own, or someone else's time. Is this time better spent gaining a few quick wins, which then 'buys' time to get the big wins, or should you go straight for the big wins, understanding that it will take time? This is a question for you as an individual, but I for one, always recommend getting a few manageable wins, and then moving onto the bigger wins.

The one thing we can say is that keyphrase research will make or break more online marketing campaigns than anything else in terms of getting the right people to your website. Once you have the list of key phrases, you can weave these into your website. There are differing views on whether key phrases should drive page content or whether page content should drive the use of key phrases. I would suggest it is a mix of the two.

Whilst you should not build a website simply to attract visitors, this has to be a part of the strategy and to suggest otherwise would be foolish. My advice is to decide prior to the exercise, what pages you need and the layout of the pages in relation to each other. You should then try to weave the key phrases throughout the content up to and not beyond the point whereby the text is distorted by the use of the key phrases.

At no point should the message on the page be adversely affected by the use of keywords to get people to the page. Without repeating the point too much, you should only be interested in attracting visitors that will ultimately convert. If your pages are 'stuffed' with key phrases, you will put people off and conversions will be low.

Competitor analysis

It is amazing how many times, people go full steam ahead and find only after spending thousands of pounds and countless hours that they have a competitor that they never knew about.

Often companies provide a list of their competitors and a list of what they like from the competitors site. The list is provided as a checklist of what they would like to be included in their own site. I call this a 'me too' list. Without realising it, you can very easily look at the project from the angle of 'I would like to be as good as they are'. This seems quite a small ambition to me.

It is vital to your success that you look at your competitors, but as much as it is to find out what good ideas they have, you also need to look at what bad ideas they have had. Also, who are your competitors?

You will typically know a handful of the ones you do battle with on a day to day basis. The one's who pitch against you, but online, they may be different. As you start to search for the wide range of key phrases that you have identified, you will see names appearing that you may not have encountered before. These guys are your competitors.

Imagine from a prospects view. They search for a certain subject; something that you supply. The first time they encounter you, you will be pitched against your online competition, not your regular offline competition. They may be the same, but it is up to you to find out and find out you must. Once you find them, make a list and start to analyse what they do. This alone will save you from making expensive mistakes.

Perform keyphrase research on them! Work out what terms they are using and how. Are they using keywords across the pages? What about the page title. The filename (the piece of the address after the domain name e.g. urbanmedia.co.uk/**internet-marketing**.aspx)

Guitar Lessons going FREE to all who will listen!

Musician and writer of a popular music tuition series has decided it would be a great idea to develop video tutorials and sell online. With a large existing customer base, it would seem this new medium would be an obvious move.

Research showed that the biggest competition would not come from other tuition providers, but the video website; YouTube.

During the research, it was discovered that many otherwise 'unknown' and previously considered 'amateur' musicians were providing a wide range of self labelled 'how to' style video tutorials for free through YouTube.

Whilst the difference in quality was evident, consumers were proving to be more interested in the content than the quality. What initially seemed like 'no competition' had now changed to 'heavily competitive'.

What is their lead generation strategy? Do they have clear calls to action? Do they have a 'sign up to our newsletter or even better, a sign up to our top tips? Are the pages clear? Do they have a good way of simplifying complex information? There are lots of questions you need to ask about the pages you navigate through on their website. What did you like? What did you not like? Now get a non biased contact to help. What do they think?

Turn your attention to their visitor attraction techniques. Are they coming up for a variety of key phrases? You can also see who links to each competitor. This will help you to gain valuable links to your website. Google has tools for this as do many SEO tool websites. http://siteexplorer.search.yahoo.com is another tool; this time from Yahoo. Use the 'inlinks' link to get a full list of sites linking to your competitor.

Take a look at their social media. Do they have a Twitter account? Is it current? Did they set it up but can't find useful information to share? Again, keep looking for the good things they do and also the bad. What is your angle? If you have to beat them, which you do, then how will you do it?

Then, once you have gone through all of this, summarise. You will have gathered lots of information and you have to make it useful. Remember, you are not trying to create a new version of what your competitors have already done. This is a 'me too' website and does not position you any better than your competitors. I encourage clients to reconsider what a website even is. You can't do this if you are constantly looking back to what your competitors do. The purpose of the exercise is to learn from their mistakes and stimulate good ideas. You then move on from that point. Not simply create a site based on the good and avoiding the bad.

Natural optimisation

Once you have done all of this and decided upon your site structure and messages etc. you are ready to optimise your pages to achieve high 'natural' rankings across the various search engines. To do this, you will need to work on both 'on page' and 'off page' elements. In the next sections, we will explore some of the main requirements to achieve the high positions you will undoubtedly desire!

There are many small elements that will provide you with an advantage over your online competition in relation to search engine position. I have highlighted some key areas in the following 'on page' and 'off page' sections. Before we explore them, I should explain how the listings are created and how on page elements are affected by the search engine algorithm.

The Search Engine Algorithm

The algorithm (maths based equation), is a very powerful formulae for working out what pages are most relevant for the search term that a searcher has entered into the search box. The algorithm changes over time as the search engines continue to improve their listings. I always encourage people to understand the business model for Google as a way to understand how the algorithm has to work.

Google (and the other search engines) are businesses. It makes money from people paying for advertising alongside its natural listings. They have to ensure that their natural listings are extremely relevant to gain the highest number of searchers. Then, and only if the results are consistently high quality, they have a huge audience and by the sheer volume, they will get sufficient numbers of searchers (around 30% of clicks) using the paid listings.

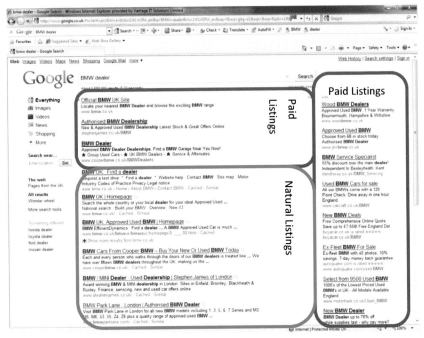

'Google Search Listings'

The way a search engine achieves relevant results is by mathematically analysing the content of a page. This is the only way a computer programme can. The relevance of page content is assessed in relation to the term used to search. Let's take a basic look at this to highlight.

If I search for BMW and your website has BMW as the entire domain name, file name, title, H1 tag, Alt Tag etc. etc., then you will be showing Google (if it believed you!) that you are 100% relevant to my search. If however, you had 'BMW Dealer' in all of these places, you are now 50% relevant. 'BMW Dealer Birmingham' would show up as 33% relevant and so on. Equally if you had 'BMW' as your term and I had searched 'BMW Dealer' you can start to understand how this would work. You would be 50% relevant etc.

This highlights the importance of keyphrase research. We need to know what people search for and be 100% relevant for the terms that we want to achieve high positions for. This leads me onto the subject of placing lots of key words or phrases on each page. This is a practise still carried out, but using the paragraph above, you can see what would happen to the relevance of the terms that a searcher had used. When you understand the basic principles of how a search engine has to derive its listings, you can begin to build page content and keyphrase strategies around these principles.

Knowing that the search results are made up in this way, we simply need to put 'bigger' ticks in every box that the search engine is looking for. This way, regardless of what weighting is given by a search engine to a particular element, you will beat the competition. This is easier for 'on page' than 'off page' as we will see in the coming sections. However, it is possible over time, to beat any competition. The consideration is not whether you can beat a competitive page, it is how much time/money you can invest in the process and therefore whether other phrases may be more cost effective.

First, let's look at 'on page' elements that gain high search positions.

On Page

'On page' methods of optimising your pages for higher search engines refer to the various changes you can make to the actual web pages themselves. Some of these are easier than others and if possible, to achieve the best results, you should have your pages built by a team that understand search engine optimisation. This does not mean by someone who does search engine optimisation. The 2 skills; building web pages and internet marketing are very different. Your success in this area may well be a reflection of whether you assigned the task to the right team.

For this reason, I have included a section at the back of the book on choosing a partner. It is possible to find companies that have specialists in a variety of fields all working for the same company and therefore understanding not only their specialism, but also how it affects other requirements. More of this towards the end of the book!

Domain Name

It stands to reason that the most permanent feature of a website should have a high level of importance within the algorithm. The domain name cannot easily be changed, so it is about as permanent as you can get. If you are a local building supplies company in Leeds called Smith and Jones, you are likely to register the name 'smithandjones.co.uk' as your domain name. Now think back to the way a search engine works. Should a searcher look for 'smith and jones', you will have achieved a big tick.

Chances are a searcher looking for the products that you sell would be more inclined to search for 'Leeds building supplies' or 'Leeds building materials' etc. What you could and indeed should consider is the use of your keyphrase within the domain name. If your domain name was leedsbuildingsupplies.co.uk, you will have scored the same big tick, but for a keyphrase that is more likely to generate the kind of traffic to your website that you are looking for.

File names

After the domain name itself, follows the filename of the pages within your website. You may well have noticed pages like yourcompanyname.co.uk/services.html. The 'services.html' part is the filename. This is just the same as if you had a folder called My Documents and a file called 'Our Services.docx'. The address is likely to be c:\\My Documents\Our Services.docx. All files have names. Search engines look within the filename to see if any key phrases are to be found. Rather than using say 'contact.html', try using 'contact-leeds-building-supplies.html'. You can extend this to cover your entire product range on a number of pages within your website.

Title tag

Look at the very top of the browser and you will see the title of any web page that you are accessing. This title is different to the actual filename. It is a common place for bad search engine optimisation techniques to be used. This is where you often see 'product1 | product2 | product3 | product4' etc. think back to what we have discussed on 'relevance' and you will see that if someone is searching for 'product4', yes, you will be listed, but where? Your relevance will be dramatically reduced with every additional key phrase added.

Meta tags

The Meta 'keywords' and 'description' tags were once the key to search engine optimisation. They told search engines what the page content was based on. The big problem was; since they are invisible to the site visitor, you could easily mislead your site visitor and this is not great for the search engines. Search engines need to list quality sites and by using Meta tags to list sites, they are easily tricked.

Let's consider how this could be misused. You create a page to sell a pyramid selling scheme. The page is 100% geared towards selling the benefits of getting rich quick and building a team of people who earn money for you while you sleep or even better, sail your luxury yacht! The Meta tags on the other hand are all about investments and investing. When I search, I am looking for investment opportunities. The pages that my favourite search engine delivers me are not exactly what I was expecting.

We have already looked at the importance of quality listings, so it is easy to see why the search engines now pay little attention to the Meta keywords and description tags especially if they contain terms that are not spread across the site within the visible elements.

It is worth mentioning though that the description tag is used within the listing even if not in the algorithm that positions your page within the listing. When you see the listings (e.g. Google), you get Blue, Black and Green text. The Blue is the page Title. The Black is the Meta Description. The Green is the page domain and filename. As you cast your eye on the top 5 listings, the one that clearly contains what you are looking for without any extra confusion will be the one you are most likely to click. This does not always mean number one on the list.

H tags (H1, H2, H3)

It is the 'on page' elements that are visible that will continue to be given a higher priority. These visible elements can't be cheated. If they are on the page, they must be relevant to the reader.

The 'H' tags are a series of tags that can tell search engines and (visually) users alike, what is important on the particular page. The heading (H) tags are given a priority order; H1, H2, H3 and H4. You should ensure a variation upon your key phrases exist within the H tags. If you simply repeat the same key phrase in all of the heading tags, this is easily seen as un-natural and therefore mechanically engineered which means 'spam'.

Let's use the term 'Leeds Building Supplies' as our main key phrase. You can see how we could vary this by using

H1   Leeds Building Supplies
H2   Building Supplies

H3   Leeds supplier of building materials

H4   Building materials supplied to the Leeds area

You can see how this would help your site to be found for a variation of terms based on the main term. Remember, not everyone will search using the same exact search term. Your job is to find out what the best term is through keyphrase research and find one or two variations. You can then thread the variations around the main term as seen here with H tags.

Alt tags

Alt tags are designed to be used by the visually impaired to 'see' what is contained within an image. They are the text boxes that appear when you

move your mouse over an image. As you can see with the image to the right, you can easily add 'search friendly' terms to these tags and still maintain compliance with the Disability Discrimination Act (DDA) in terms of the usefulness (descriptiveness) of the tag for a visually impaired user. Remember at the beginning of the section on natural optimisation I aired a warning that the developer you use should be a developer who understands matters outside their specialism. Not everyone is a DDA specialist, but an awareness of the subject is vital.

Keyphrase density (the words)

The main area of any page will be the text on the page. The text on the page has so much to achieve. It is responsible for converting visitors into customers as well as getting the visitor there in the first place by ensuring the key phrases you have identified to 'attract' visitors are spread consistently and effectively throughout the actual page with the correct density.

Remember, the algorithm is mathematical. The algorithm will search the number of words used on a page and work out how many of these make up the term that a searcher has used to find your listing. Even more importantly, the search engine is able to prioritise not only phrases within the H tags, but those that have special dressing such as bold and italics. The algorithm can even weight more heavily words within the first paragraphs or number of words.

To make things worse, the algorithm is a moving target. So how is it possible to beat the system? Well, firstly, do not try to beat the system! The search engine is only trying to place the best, most relevant content at the top. As a searcher, do you want poor quality content at the top that has been cleverly engineered to 'beat the system'? Chances are your answer is 'no, except when it comes to my pages!!' This is normal, but not helpful. The only way to win long term with the search engines is to give them what they want. That way, they win, you win and ultimately the searcher wins.

Providing quality, relevant and key phrase rich content will generate you far more business than any shortcuts will. You will get out what you put in. How true is that in life and every other area of your business? The web is no different. Build a strategy around quality content and you will win in terms of search engine optimisation.

Off Page

Of course there are other less major factors that affect on page optimisation, but these change often and are best left to the professionals. If you understand the areas covered above, you will be a lot further than your competitors.

It is vital that you also understand how 'off page' factors will affect your listings also. A large part of the listings are made up of the off page factors. These take longer to establish and are probably a more reliable source of guidance for the search engine. For this reason it is understandable that the search engines look to the 'wider community' for input.

Link Strategy

The biggest area of 'off page' natural optimisation is link strategy. I believe this has a large crossover with Social Media, since a good link strategy campaign will include building certain social media 'pages' as strong links back to the main website.

To understand link strategy, we need to understand the following;

- Links; a link from your web page to another web page
- Reciprocal Links; a link from your page to another page where the receiving page also links back to your page
- Backwards Links; a link to your web page from another web page

The three types of links are not the same and should be understood. For years, site owners built pages of links to other sites in the belief that this helped their web site somehow. This is misguided and does not help your website at all.

Then, we had 'link farms'. These were sites that would place a link to your website from theirs. This was either for a fee (which in certain circumstances could possibly help) or for a link back to them. This type of reciprocal link has limited value. If you think about this for a minute, it is easy to see how using reciprocal links you could build up your own network of sites and the 'vote' that we will talk about, from one site to another is meaningless.

A backwards link is different to the other 2 as it is a 'vote' of confidence from another page to your page, without any seen benefit to the 'voting' page. Let's explore this. If you had a website and understood that linking to other websites didn't help your site, which sites would you link to? Firstly, it is likely to be very few. Then, should you choose to, the quality of the page would have to be good for you to link to that page and send your valued visitor to another site. You are passing on a 'vote' of confidence for that page.

Google takes this a step further in its algorithm. The Page Rank system devised by Google places a rank on every page it has indexed in its database. The old one man one vote is out! If you have a link to your page from a page with an existing high page rank, it will count for more than the same link if it was from a page with low page rank. Think about this for a minute.

If I associate with the people that are not up to much and they recommend me, how much value do you place on their recommendation? Conversely, if I associate with the high flyers of business and commerce, what weight do you apply to their recommendation of me? Why should a search engine work any different? And that is why it doesn't. You need links from lots of high page rank web pages.

Notice I keep using the term pages. A website is a collection of pages and each one stands on its own merits. A link to your homepage does not directly benefit your services page. We regularly seek links for a wide variety of our pages, not just a link direct to the home page. There is another reason why though.

Imagine I am a surgeon. You speak to a plumber and he tells you I am a really good surgeon. If the plumber has any credibility, this will indeed help your view of me. What, however if you spoke to another surgeon and he told you just how good I was. Assuming the other surgeon also had credibility, his relevance to the recommendation adds a lot of weight. This is also true in link strategy.

So, the best link is where the content on the page that contains the link is similar to the content on the page receiving the link. It is where the link text (the bit you click or the alt tag on an image) carries the key phrase that has been used to optimise the page that the link takes you to. Everything is relevant. Never forget the importance of relevance.

Domain Age

Another part of the Page Rank calculation (in fact its own mini algorithm) is the length of time a domain has existed for and been registered for. Google doesn't want to create listings that are full of 'page not found'. If the site has existed for a while and will be around for a while longer, it is a 'safer' bet.

Google Maps

For a long time, the search engines have realised the future is in localised search. You can create instant top of page one listing using Google Local or Google Maps. When a searcher uses your location in their search term for example 'Leeds Building Supplies', your listing will appear with a map of the town and you will appear as one of the 'pins' in the map.

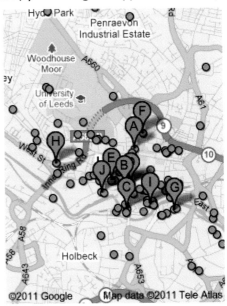

This is not an alternative to gaining your own first page listings as many people are still not used to the listings next to the map and people do not always use the geographic term in their search. It is a very quick way to get on page one though and should be part of your activity.

Social Media

Social Media I believe overlaps with Link Strategy and therefore I have included a paragraph here. We will discuss Social Media in its own section to follow. This paragraph should simply highlight that there are many sites that allow you to build 'fan' or 'company' pages. These pages, due to their connectivity to the main social media site that they belong to, do rank very quickly and very well. This should form part of your link strategy and would involve building 'profile' pages on sites such as 'Squidoo' and 'Hub Pages'

Paid advertising

There is a wide selection of paid advertising options available. They can be split into 3 basic types;

- Banner advertising on another person's website
- Affiliate schemes
- Pay per Click systems

Banner Adverts

Banner adverts are typically placed on high traffic websites such as industry specific forums. The basic principal is similar to that of a search engine's business model. The site generates traffic through having a compelling reason for visitors to repeat visit and as a result is able to sell space on its pages. The sheer volume of traffic supports the advertisers need to have their banner shown (impressions) and clicked on (clicks).

Care should be taken when planning to buy banner space that the traffic is highly targeted. Also, be sure what you are buying. Impressions are typically understood as 'views' of your banner. You may need a lot of those to create a click, and a lot of clicks to create a customer. Know your numbers from top to bottom. Where possible, buy clicks, not impressions. If the seller of the banner space becomes vague as to what they call a click/impression, ensure you get whatever it is you are buying in writing.

Affiliate schemes

Affiliate schemes are in common use, but you may not have considered them. Quite often, people will have books from Amazon on their website. This is an affiliate scheme. For every person that clicks on the book and buys from Amazon, they pay the affiliate a commission.

Later in the book, we will look at Automated Marketing. In particular, I use the system that I designed from scratch due to a lack of such a system. This system called Highway, has an affiliate scheme. On the highwaycrm.com website it is referred to as a reseller programme, but they mean the same thing. When anyone signs up to be a reseller, they are given tools to promote the system. Each 'tool' carries their unique reseller code and any sales that come through their activity will produce residual income through commission for that reseller.

It may seem an 'off the wall' suggestion, but running a reseller or affiliate programme may be something that you could use in your business. This method of paid advertising is more involved to setup and works better for some products/services than others, but you shouldn't rule it out. Remember, you would only pay out when you make a sale. You can therefore afford to be more generous and with less risk at the same time.

Pay per Click

Probably the most used method of paying for visitors to your website. This is understandable as it is quick to setup, without long contracts and everyone trusts a system where you only pay when you receive a click. Although, you should understand some of the basics of Pay per Click before spending too much of your limited online marketing spend.

Three of the big systems are;

Google Adwords

Probably the longest running Pay per Click system. We have already looked at where the natural listings and paid listings in Google appear on their search results page. Other search engines run similar systems and in a similar way. You enter key phrases that your adverts (text based) should be displayed for. Your adverts will then be shown when a user searches for those terms, according to the settings you have. These settings are similar to the other main systems so we will discuss these collectively.

Facebook ads

Facebook Ads can be more visual. They contain 'Body' text, but also tend to contain images. The ads are shown to users of Facebook based on keyphrases used within their profile. If you have a product for people interested in 'horse riding' and within a Facebook users profile, they have stated that they are interested in horse riding, your advert will show. Again, this is based on the settings you have chosen.

You can even base ads on personal data such as a user's birthday or relationship status. If you run a 'singles' night, your adverts do not need to be wasted on the 'married'!

LinkedIn ads

LinkedIn is the B2B (business to business) equivalent of Facebook. Once again, you can choose a variety of targeting methods. With LinkedIn, this can be based on more business related criteria such as job title or size of company. You can choose gender or age related terms, or even what LinkedIn groups they belong to.

LinkedIn is extremely powerful and the advertising system within this network of millions of business people is a great platform for business to business sales. As with all of the Pay per Click systems, you can control lots of detail, but there are some basics that apply to all.

Regardless of the system, you will want to set the amount that you are willing to pay for a single click. The Pay per Click models have increased in complexity since they were first introduced, but they work principally on an auction basis. The advert at the top is paying more than the one below and so on. Now, just to reaffirm, this is not the only way the order of the adverts are sorted, but for the purpose of understanding the basics, this is the major way.

Accuracy of the advert to the content of the page where the advert links is part of the more advanced elements of optimising your Pay per Click adverts. There are books dedicated to Google Adwords, LinkedIn adverts, Facebook Adverts and the like. If you intend to master the systems, you should stay up to date with not only these books, but regular blogs across the internet dedicated to advanced use of particular systems. What I want to achieve is to give you a simple understanding that you will remember, rather than too much detail at this point that you are more likely to not remember.

The next thing to consider is your maximum budget. This, in the early days is important. Once you have a proven model, your maximum budget, in theory should be zero or lots! It's obvious really. Is the system bringing you a return on your spend (R.O.I.)? If so, do more, if not, stop it unless you are still in the evaluation period and you know what changes you need to do next to improve the results.

Then, you will know from these 2 numbers, how many advert clicks, you will receive (budget divided by cost per click). Make sure the number is sufficient otherwise you will not be able to make sensible decisions on whether you are getting a return on your investment. You see, I have never won any money on the National Lottery. It is not the conversion rate that is bad; I have never bought a ticket. In the same way, if you receive 50 clicks and decide that you are not getting enough 'clicks' converting into visitors, make sure you are getting better than 50:1 from your other website conversions. If not, you may be about to give in too soon.

Social Media

Social Media is probably the biggest change area in online activity since the Search Engine. It is no longer 'new', but it is still very misunderstood in relation to business benefits. Despite this, there is a massive uptake in terms of business owners turning to Facebook, Twitter and LinkedIn in particular.

All three have their place in your online strategy, but there are some really obvious ground rules that are being apparently overlooked. Before going into some of the most popular (and probably, most effective) social media activities, I would like to talk through them.

Creating an integrated campaign

There is no point looking at Social Media in either an isolated way or in a fragmented way. What I mean by this is that using just one method is probably a poor use of time and running several social media activities without combining your efforts is certainly a waste of time. With that said, you may and I would suggest; should, recognise that you have different audiences on each social media site.

Your challenge is to be clear as to who is on which social media site and what 'tailored' message you want to use on that site, if the messages do indeed need to be different. If you sell products that have a business application and a personal application, you may wish to use Facebook to reach your consumer audience and LinkedIn/Twitter to reach your corporate clients. In this way, the message is tailored to the audience and instantly more 'relevant' to me; the 'would be' customer.

You will see in the following sections that social media is not just the 140 character 'tweets'. The subject covers audio, video, image and slideshows, not simply words. Remember we are living in a multimedia world. You need to communicate through a variety of media. This is just the start.

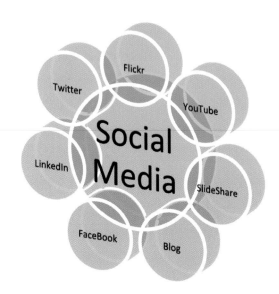

You need to have mechanisms for full communication in terms of both ways. Communication does not mean aimlessly broadcasting your message in a vague hope that someone will see it and develop a burning desire to become your next 'best customer'.

Watch the time!

One of the biggest problems I see with small businesses in particular is the phenomenon of my time does not cost me anything. I believe this to be 100% inaccurate. If you were not using that time for the activity you put into it, what could the time be used for. At its worst, you could sell that time to an employer paying you minimum wage. More relevantly, the time could be used to generate higher income opportunities or for rest.

I run a very simple exercise. It goes like this; how much is your time worth? How much time will you spend carrying out a task (in this case communicating on social media sites)? Multiply one by the other and work out the cost to you or your business of Social Media. I am not against spending the time. I am in favour of correctly budgeted social media activities. What I do say though is; the time spent on social media is not free. Dispel the myth that your 'free-time' is free time.

Recycle your material

One of the best ways to both perform an integrated campaign and save time is to recycle your content well. Not all of your 'audience' will want to watch your slideshow. Some may want to watch your video, others will prefer to print off your blog and read your valuable content later. Equally, others will want to keep 'feeding' on your snippets of information through their RSS feeder or favourite Twitter application.

Imagine this book. There is a lot of very valuable information in here. It would be very easy to break it down into bite size elements and share that through a series of still images in the style of 'thought provokers' shared on Flickr. It would then be easy to create bite size info PowerPoint slides and share them on Slideshare. I could read them over some royalty free music, using the same slides as a backdrop and I now have videos for YouTube. Naturally I would include some related blog posts and all of this would be signposted from my LinkedIn and Twitter profiles. In turn, all of this social media would direct people to my website.

If you have picked up on the message in the last paragraph, you have just received a huge, money saving, profit making plan to promote your business. Re-read the paragraph if ideas did not start flooding in as to how you could apply this format to your business.

As I write this, I have just heard that someone (they will remain nameless!) has just broken their entire book into 140 character tweets. They are broadcasting it through Twitter to be the first book shared in full over Twitter. Sounds clever, but would you read it in this way? I wouldn't either. Don't do any of this type of activity without thinking it through fully. It is not a gimmick. Or at least it shouldn't be. There is a flip side to everything. This person will soon have a lot of followers choosing to 'unfollow' and the sensible added value communication channel has been reduced.

Overview of your options

If you have decided that Social Media will form part of your online marketing, and I would suggest that in most cases, you should, then you need to know which sites suit your creativity, time and personal style. These three factors will dictate what you can or should do.

As an example, I have two clients with the same fairly high budgets and with although they would argue otherwise, very similar products. The difference that they have is their personality. What one could carry off well, the other couldn't. This is both ways. Again, they may beg to differ, but trust me, they must. You should create an online profile in keeping with your natural personality. The business persona that is; the corporate culture that planned or unplanned, you have created.

The following sections provide an overview of your 'current' options.

Facebook

Facebook is a social networking website connecting businesses and individuals online. You may already be involved with Facebook for personal use, however the most popular and efficient way of using Facebook as a business is to create a 'page'.

Facebook Pages are specifically designed for businesses, brands and organizations and therefore are not attributed to an individual. Whilst some internet marketers advocate the use of Facebook for all businesses, I disagree. If you have a consumer brand, I agree that Facebook is a great way to engage with your 'users'. If you are predominantly in the B2B space, I believe it has less use.

In fact, without sounding old fashioned, I disagree with its use to overtly promote your B2B service or product on Facebook, when the vast majority of people are on the site for social reasons. It is not that business and pleasure can't mix as I know they can. What I would say though is you can easily put people off! I have become 'non friends' with people over just these overly sales pitched postings.

They allow you to:

- Connect with your audience be it current or potential customers.
- Build your name in a new market.
- Show others a new and more personal side to your company.
- Engage in real-time conversations and discussions

You can add a range of basic company information and details. Including:

- Opening times
- Contact details
- Company description, website address.
- Photographs

On your page your will have the opportunity to create a number of photo albums.

You may wish to upload images such as:

- Company Logo
- Photos of your Staff
- Photos of your Premises
- Photos of your Products
- Events you've run/attended

You are able to start discussions, using the 'Discussions' tab. This allows you to encourage interaction between yourselves and your 'fans' as well as between fans.

You are able to add custom tabs to your page. This could range from adding a lengthy company overview to a list of sale items, details of an event, contact details for your stores/offices etc.

For larger organizations with larger budgets, they may decide to create their own Facebook application. This could be a competition app, game app etc. These applications can then be shown on the Facebook page for all to see.

When people 'Like' your page, this will show up in their news feed and will be shown to their friends. This can potentially build brand awareness and may lead to gaining more fans and on from that, more business.

You can also interact with those who like your organization/brand/company and reward them accordingly. This may be via the promotion of exclusive offers, discount codes or sharing of knowledge and information etc. This will make them feel that 'liking' your page is worthwhile.

Usefully, Facebook has an inbuilt Facebook page tracking system called 'Insights'.

This will provide you with information on:

- Page views
- Number of fans
- Removed fans
- Wall posts

You can also gather further information depending on which 'Tabs' you are using. Tabs include: Notes, Events, Photos, Discussions as well as your custom tabs or applications.

LinkedIn

LinkedIn is a social networking website targeted at businesses and therefore mainly used for professional networking.

LinkedIn is not only a great networking tool but also a useful element of internet marketing. You can edit and optimise your profile to include keyphrases and links to your website; LinkedIn has high authority in Google and therefore doing so will increase the chances of your profile appearing for your targeted keyphrases.

There is a large range of uses for LinkedIn. As such, you would expect a range of books highlighting the best uses. The uses, do change based on your requirements. If you want to keep your LinkedIn as a collection of very key contacts with high value to your network, you will 'connect' with a limited number of people. If you intend to use the system for sales or recruitment, you will go all out for gathering as many connections as you can!

I believe that every business professional should be active on LinkedIn. It is in my mind, the number one tool within social media. Just an opinion I know, but it is so powerful, whereas other systems are not designed to be 'powerful', they are designed to be easy or quick (Twitter). This doesn't mean LinkedIn is difficult, just far more comprehensive. I have outlined 4 main steps to get you started.

1. Establish Your Professional Profile

On LinkedIn there is a large range of information that can be added to your profile. As LinkedIn ranks so highly in the search engines, it is essential that you optimise the page to give yourself a positive online identity. You must make your profile public for the profile to be found in Google.

Golf day link leads to increased business

Office furniture sales rep finds benefits in the 'LinkedIn' social network after attending a recent Golf Day. Ensuring she had 'introductory' chats with fellow golfers, [Lucy] then went outside the time constraints of the golf day to connect with the golfers on LinkedIn.

Following some initial conversations, [Lucy] had seen that the people she had met were linked to some ideal prospects for her office furniture business. Using the 'joint' connection, she requested an introduction to those '2nd degree' connections.

Her new found golfing friends, were more than happy to make introductions where they felt both people would benefit.

As a result, the 'connector' gained credibility and [Lucy]'s company got more from that golf day than any other event they had done before!

You will also see on your profile, the 'percentage' that you have completed. You should get your profile 100% complete. It is worth the effort. Once completed, you should keep this up to date. You will see that every time you update your profile, a message is sent out to your connections letting them know you have an updated profile.

Tips to make full use of your profile:

- Upload a professional picture
- Give relevant information about yourself
- A quick engaging description will promote both you and your business
- Make use of anchor text and links to your website.
- Include your company keywords within your profile
- Ensure you add 'previous work places and schools'
- This could potentially bring new clients not only from old friends and colleagues but also the people they now know.

2. Connect and Keep In touch

LinkedIn also gives you the opportunity to remain in close contact with a range of contacts you may have otherwise lost communication with. Individuals are constantly moving or changing their phone numbers, LinkedIn provides a safe and professional online portal for you to connect and remain up to date with everyone's location and details.

This may help in the future to bring new customers or business opportunities. You will often see now, that emails are sent from within LinkedIn.

3. Find or Provide Answers

Whilst using LinkedIn you can also make the most of expert advice. When you and your colleagues do not know the answer to something you can pose the question to professionals through the use of groups and the Answers tool.

The LinkedIn Search will allow you to search the network by name, title, company, location and other keywords providing you with the perfect contact to resolve your problem.

Providing answers also shows your professional knowledge. It is a good idea to regularly look for questions that you can answer. The main ethos behind a successful LinkedIn strategy is about adding value, just like any other online marketing campaign.

Asking questions or providing answers can also provide you with useful connections for the future and helps you to meet new and experienced business people.

4. Explore Opportunities

Using LinkedIn effectively can provide you with a huge amount of benefits. In my internet marketing seminars, I tell the story about the girl who taught me to use LinkedIn. It wasn't that I didn't know how to use the 'system', but I hadn't realised the full potential. After meeting at a golf event, she connected to me on LinkedIn (see the previous 'pop out box'. Noticing that we work for a commercial estate agent, she asked me to connect her to my contact as she had a service of value.

Since there was a genuine synergy, I was happy to connect the two and they now have a business relationship that would not have existed if she had not understood one of the key uses of LinkedIn. There are many opportunities if you look. For example new career opportunities, winning new clients, building relationships with existing clients, sales leads, recruiting, advice and expertise from leading professionals and more!

This is just the start. LinkedIn can provide you with invaluable connections along with acting as an excellent internet marketing tool. It has tools for you to promote events (our Internet Marketing Seminars are always published on LinkedIn) and its 'message' wall, can be shared with your Twitter account to save you sending messages twice, which brings me nicely onto Twitter itself.

Twitter

Twitter is a micro blogging site where users can share 'tweets' of up to 140 characters. Not much of a message, but Twitter is used by a huge range of people from celebrities to businesses or even just individuals who wish to communicate with others using the website.

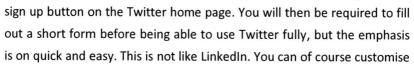

These tweets can contain information on a range of topics. It is an excellent tool for companies to use when trying to interest potential clients and entice them to their website for further follow through.

To use Twitter you will first need to make an account. This can be done simply by clicking on the sign up button on the Twitter home page. You will then be required to fill out a short form before being able to use Twitter fully, but the emphasis is on quick and easy. This is not like LinkedIn. You can of course customise your 'profile', but Twitter in the style of its 140 character limit, is designed to be easy.

This simplicity has led to a lot of other Twitter applications. These applications allow you to do 'more' on Twitter. These may be pre scheduling some 'tweets' or managing more than one twitter account from one application/login.

Once you have an account you can begin 'Tweeting'. To post your own tweets simply type the message in the box at the top of your page.

You may also wish to 'retweet' a message that someone else has posted and you support. This retweet function is the power tool in Twitter. We have spoken about 'Tribes', and retweeting fits directly into this. Imagine sending out a message to your 'fan base'. Twitter lets you do this easily. But now, imagine your fan base sending that message on to their entire fan base' and so on. One message tweeted to 100 people can soon be viewed by 1,000's of people.

Similarly you can reply to a tweet posted by another individual. This is where I see the real power of Twitter. The art of using Twitter properly is to engage in communication with your 'followers' or people who use your name in their tweets. Used this way, Twitter takes customer service to a whole new level. You can now step in when a customer has something slightly unfavourable to say about your products/services. You have a chance to put things right. When your act of putting things right is done in public, if you do it right, you will win a lot of fans.

One of the reasons why Twitter is such a useful tool is because of the freedom you have with what you write. It gives businesses a chance to show themselves on a more personal level. However it is also wise to consider the fact you are still marketing yourselves.

If you are stuck, consider tweeting:

- Company updates
- Things that interest you
- Articles relating to your industry
- Links to your new web pages/new product info
- Promotional Offers
- Top Tips

Before signing up, think about your Username. Ensure you create a username that is relevant to your company as others may search for your company name in order to find your profile.

Incorporate your company branding. As part of your profile set up you can incorporate a unique background, make the most of this by creating a quirky and memorable design fitting with your branding.

Integrate your Twitter with your company website. Incorporate your tweets with your website using a twitter widget. This creates an up to date feed on your website along with attracting current and potential customers to follow you on Twitter.

Tweet regularly and wisely. Tweeting regularly keeps your name out there and prevents followers from becoming disinterested. Ensure you post relevant and appropriate content at least a few times each week.

Remember, tweeting is good, but just like on LinkedIn, conversations are the secret. If you believe that you will collect an endless supply of business just by bleating on to people rather than tweeting with people, it will not work. Entire conversations, build value and this could become the face of a much wider, very successful social media campaign.

YouTube

YouTube is a free video sharing website on which any user can upload, view and comment on videos. There is a great range of videos on YouTube; both Commercial and Leisure. Whilst many use the website to put up funny clips or to watch their favourite music video, there is a massive business opportunity. The site is being used more and more by people looking to find out about a range of services.

Examples of YouTube videos are:

- TV clips and adverts
- Music Videos
- Movie Trailers
- Video Blogs
- Amateur videos
- Professional video guides
- Video Testimonials

Using YouTube is very simple. The first step you need to take is to create an account. From there, businesses should create a 'channel'. See this as your own 'On Demand' TV channel. Once you have your channel, upload videos relevant to your products and services.

You can see from the previous list the type of video that you can upload. It would be a good idea to look around existing videos in your subject area by searching for your products (by description!)

As a company you may wish to make your YouTube channel or a few of the videos private. This means that the exposure of the video is limited to only you and 50 other users which you invite to watch the video. It also means that the video will not appear on your channel or within any search results or playlists. You simply send a link to the people you wish to watch the video. This is great for internal training.

Make your video Interesting. Is your video something that audiences will find interesting and enjoy watching? If not, don't upload it. It is better to have fewer more interesting videos than a high amount of videos that audiences will switch off. It also makes audiences more likely to watch future videos.

Make your video appropriate for everyone who may be interested in your products/services. Make sure your video will appeal to all audiences, remember not to include anything that may

A perfect Blend of creativity attracts thousands!

Using the 'Science Abuse' style comedy; household appliance company 'Blendtec' have created quite a following. Their www.willitblend.com website is a 'smash hit' and definitely 'Top of the Pots'.

On the site, they attempt, with a lot of success to blend a variety of objects that you would not typically see inside your food blender. Take the iPhone 4 or iPad for example! In their aptly labelled 'don't try this at home' section, there is no end of fun.

Meanwhile, in their 'do try this at home' section, the website displays their very 'sensible' side, with the usual array of blended food recipes.

One thing for sure, I know more about Blendtec as a result. Next time I want a blender, you can guess where I will be going.

offend specific genders or ethnic groups etc.

Show your personality. Like other social media devices, YouTube is a chance for you to show a more informal side. Your videos can therefore be personable and on a more friendly level allowing customers to see the real you! Remember, if your company image is not comedic, don't be funny. If you are creative, show it!

Share your video on Twitter. Make sure you post a link to your video on your Twitter account. If you are using Facebook, do the same. This will attract more viewers and also shows your customers another side to your business.

There is a common theme here, where you create content for Social Media, use it across all platforms. Create quality content. The production quality should be consistent with your company, but you do not have to use the film crew from Disney Studios to put quality content onto YouTube!

Flickr
Flickr is an online photo management and sharing application powered by Yahoo. The site has two main objectives. To help people make their photos and videos available to others and to enable new ways of organising photos and videos

When you first use Flickr, again you should create a profile. You can then import contacts. You can also begin to upload photos. As a business it is important to think about what is appropriate to your audience. You may want your staff Christmas party on there, but is that useful for a potential client? However, before you bin the idea, it may have a benefit in recruitment. You need to consider how you will 'sort' your pictures.

Whatever you do, share quality photos or images. To get noticed your photos need to stand out and be high quality. So even if you have decided to have a 'join us' category to show off your 'happy team', make sure you thoroughly check the images for quality and 'editorial' control!

When using Flickr, the thing that has to capture the audience first will be simply a thumbnail, when you are cropping and editing photos ensure to bare this in mind. What looks good in 'full size' may not work as a thumbnail.

Tagging your photos well, will bring them up in the most appropriate search terms and help people to find your images. Try to use popular search terms. Tie this in with your keyphrase research. You will know what terms you want to appear in the search engines. In fact, getting your images seen in the search engines could be as beneficial to you as a business as maintain a good Flickr profile itself.

Joining and contributing to groups gets your name out there and allows you to be part of a bigger community. Remember, Social Media is all about contributing to communities. This seems like a drain on your time and indeed I believe you need to assess time in against results out. This is why you should use similar content across your Social Media campaigns.

Incorporate your blog with Flickr to broadcast your photos to an even wider audience. Both should also be updated regularly to keep interest. Use 'Twitpic' to share pictures on Twitter.

I think that using Flickr within your social media activity holds some excellent opportunities, but it is the medium that I also believe needs the most creative thought.

Here are a couple of ideas;

- Get staff to take pictures when they are working together outside of the office. This is great for recruitment when you see a happy team working outside of the roles where they 'have' to. This could be at work functions or on CSR projects such as painting the local nursery wall!
- Create 'thought provoker' images from your PowerPoint slides. If you have the slides anyway, re-use the key points, save as pictures (jpeg) and upload!

Why not engage your team members and even those around you in brainstorming what you could use Flickr for.

Slideshare

SlideShare is an online portal on which you can upload, watch and comment on a variety of presentations. It is the largest online community for sharing presentations. SlideShare allows individuals to share ideas, conduct research, connect with others and generate leads.

Anyone can view presentations that interest them, download the file and use the information in it for their own work. You also have the option to upload their files privately as with the videos in YouTube.

Whilst the majority of the content is in Slideshow (PowerPoint style) format, you can upload a range of documents to SlideShare including:

- PowerPoint Presentations
- Pdf's
- Video's
- Webinars

Recently voted one of the top 10 resources for education and e-learning, SlideShare It is used by many big organisations including the US Government! It is a safe and efficient place to upload your presentations and documents. Making quality content available through SlideShare positions you as an expert in your field and adds a lot of weight to your standing in social media circles.

Using SlideShare is easy. To view presentations you will not need an account, simply search the website using keyphrases to find relevant presentations. You may also wish to watch the featured presentations or those listed within top presentations of the day all of which are found on the homepage.

I suggest that you create an account so that you can upload your own media. Once you have a login, you will have your own profile page on which you can upload a photo of yourself / company logo and also write a short description. See the consistent theme here!

Once you have uploaded your presentations, you can then share them on other Social Media devices within a few seconds. At the side of the presentation, there is a series of buttons to share across sites such as Facebook, Twitter, WordPress and Blogger.

To make the presentations most effective for your company there are a few things you may wish to consider:

- Make the presentations eye catching and memorable
- With so many presentations in one place you have to make yours stand out from the crowd, get creative!
- Incorporate your company branding
- This may even provide you with new business.

- No information overload
- For the most part presentations should consist of short quick facts.
- Share, share, share!
- Once you've posted your video make sure you share it with everyone whether this is through your blog or another social media device.

As we continue to 'need' more information, the thought leaders will be the real business winners. We have looked at a lot of social media outlets, and this list is not exhaustive, it is just representative. It is not that you can only put one type of media on each say video to YouTube, but they do all have a focus.

With Slideshare, you have the opportunity to collate a lot of your 'knowledge' and prove to the outside world that you or your business is an entity worth doing business with.

Blogging

A blog is a place either on your website or an external blogging portal such as 'e:blogger' where businesses can interact on a more personable level.

It is an extremely useful online marketing tool as it helps build your companies online presence. Through creating interesting posts and discussions you are building a new and interesting relationship with customers and directing more traffic through your website. The challenge for businesses is often what to write. After all, we are not all journalists and coming up with regular new ideas can seem daunting. Once you get into running a blog, you will find it is not as challenging as you first thought. The benefits can be huge too.

You will not have to generate all of the content yourself, as there are lots of interesting changes in every industry that you must have an opinion on. Let's take Accountants, every time legislation changes; they have a supply of fresh material for their blog. IT companies get even more opportunity to do this. Their industry changes monthly!

On top of this, we can all;

- Post information about our business
- Post information about successes your staff have achieved
- Post related articles, written by experts related to you
- Add advice and tips on top of your 'Expert' opinion.
- Watch your competitors blog for ideas
- Invite your audience to discuss issues

Business Blogger gains Newspaper Column

To many, writing a 'blog' may seem a waste of time. Not to one business owner who has started a cult following. His recent 'blog' telling the story of how a business can be assessed quite simply by their choice of Loo Roll (?) caused quite a stir.

Whilst the entrepreneur responsible had a serious message, he had used humour to put across his point in a series of blog 'posts' designed to get fellow business people to look at how they can improve their businesses.

Intrigued, the 'Business monthly' picked up on the posts and asked the comical business 'writer' to create a monthly column.

This has led to a cult following of other businesses that are exposed to his company's high standards, the rewards are coming in!

When planning and running your blog, keep the posts short and with a clear message. See the post as the start of a conversation. People do not have the time to read long blog posts. Keeping your posts short and relevant will help to ensure people will continue to read your posts.

As with the other Social Media sites, you can be informal, whilst not being inappropriate. Remember the conversational style of your business and make sure this comes through in your blog posts. Speak directly to your avatar. They are the target for all of your communications.

Include photos in your blog posts. Dry text will make for a far less interesting read. Consider a newspaper with no pictures. This would be the same as a blog without images. In the same way, if you have a post to get onto your blog and you do not have a picture that is ok. Remember, not all newspaper articles have pictures. The idea here is that you need to break up your text content with pictures. Don't let this control whether you post a blog post. Just make sure you don't have post after post without images.

There are different ideas on whether you should put the blog on your website or run it separately. The truth is it depends what you are trying to achieve. Ideally, you want to build the blog function into your website as search engines will see regular fresh content appearing on your website (domain).

If however you need inbound links, I believe the best way is to include the blog on your website by incorporating an external blog system into your site. This is one for your developers, but the basic explanation is that you will run a separate blog using a tool such as Google's 'Blogger'. They will then create a 'window' on your web page to show the blogger page. This should be fairly seamless. It isn't as visually pleasing as having a blog function built directly on your website, but it is a lot more cost effective and you get a lot 'backlink' benefit from this method.

There has been a tendency to use blogging software to build entire websites. After all, you can have a full 'content managed' solution free of charge. Whilst I can see the appeal, like everything in life and business, you get what you pay for. Using blogging software as a 'website' is similar to publishing your LinkedIn profile or Facebook fan page as your website address. It works, but what does it say about your business? You need to consider the whole process. What do you want out of it? You can't scrimp on what you invest and expect to reap on the return. As they say; 'you reap what you sow'. You should be wise with whom you spend your budget with and how you spend it, but to believe that you can build a business on 'Free Stuff' is frankly, quite foolish.

So, in a nutshell, use an external blogging tool where appropriate, but do not try to stretch it beyond what it is.

Summary

We have discussed a lot of social media applications. In summary, you have to find the mix that works for you in relation to time and cash resource. You should also of course understand how you are achieving a return in cash terms. Although it seems like a lot, there are a lot of tools to save time by 'recycling' content. This is not cheating; it is simply delivering your valuable knowledge content in a range of formats so that your intended recipient can digest in a way that suits them.

More Visitors!

Quick Recap

- ✓ Research the terms that will deliver the most relevant visitors
- ✓ Look at what your online competition are doing
- ✓ Do not try to keyword 'stuff'
- ✓ Go for less competitive keyphrases first and then aim high
- ✓ Understand the basics of how Google's Algorithm works
- ✓ Remember Search Engines are businesses
- ✓ High 'natural' listings are a result of on and off page work
- ✓ Try a range of paid advertising to 'test' a market
- ✓ Assess which areas you will find your 'Avatar'
- ✓ Create an integrated Social Media campaign
- ✓ Mix Natural Optimisation, Paid Listings and Social Media
- ✓ Measure the amount of time and money spent
- ✓ If you would not pay me to do it, question whether you should!
- ✓ Successful Social Media uses recycled material well
- ✓ Social Media is about conversation, not broadcast
- ✓ Whatever you do, create a holistic approach

After each Chapter, we will have discussed a lot of idea changing topics. They will apply to you differently depending on your exact requirements in relation to budget, industry, approach and more. This page is for you to write any ideas that have come to you whilst reading the last chapter. If it is blank and you have nothing to add, re-read the chapter! This time, think of each section in relation to your business.

Convert

If you can't convert your existing website visitors, then there is little point getting more people to come to your website. In fact, it would be easy for me to build an argument based on the theory that you only get one chance to make a first impression, to say that you should not allow any more visitors to your website until you work out why they are not converting.

There are a range of reasons why some websites convert a high number of visitors and some simply do not. Some of the reasons are outside of your control in terms of online marketing. They are down to factors such as level of competition, brand awareness and even industry, or profile of your prospects.

You need to look at the things you can alter. This chapter deals with these items. They are critical to your online success. They are also relatively simple. It is therefore surprising that if you were to take a look around at a wide range of websites, how often you will see these elements missing from websites that 'look' the part.

Remember your Avatar

Before you begin to put in place some of the physical elements that your website needs to include, you need to remember exactly who it is you are trying to attract. We looked in the planning section 'Before you begin', at your avatar. In fact we discussed both your ideal prospect avatar and your avatar of the person you do not want. You should bring the person(s) back to mind now as you begin to create pages that convert. Getting higher conversion rates is only a true success if you attract and convert the right new clients.

Navigation

First on the agenda is the simplicity of your navigation. Do not try to win design awards for the next best 'funky' navigation system, just make it easy. Is there a standard way used by all sites within your industry? If so, this is not the place to be revolutionary unless the standard way we refer to is bad. If it is bad, then you have license to re-think. If it works, your opportunity is in how you layout your website structure.

In terms of site structure, I mean how pages link to each other. In the simplest format, you have one long list of all your pages. This is probably impractical. You will need to group them. So, you end up with a category called 'services' for example. This is good, but could it be better? Are your services sub grouped when you refer to them in your business? I know for example that we offer three services all within the web design field in terms of how a client sees this 'web design field'.

Our three service offerings are Website Production, Online Marketing and Bespoke Applications. They are not the actual services though, they are three sub categories. Within each one, there are more details to be shared. Let's take online marketing; this can be described as natural optimisation, paid advertising and social media. Again, you could break them down further. Under 'Natural Optimisation' we could highlight Key Phrase research, Competitor Analysis, On Page Amendments and even Off Page Amendments. Your task is to break everything you do down and work out where the natural groups are.

It is important to do this through the eyes of your avatar, not through your own eyes. You understand how it all breaks down, your avatar does not. You do not need help to find your services, your avatar does. I am sure that our avatar has no real understanding of why SEO (our avatar likes to use three letter acronyms more than we do!) does not cover social media. Often, they do not understand that a website built, is not a website optimised and that they are two different processes. We need to design our navigation in such a way that meets their needs, not ours.

Copy

Once you have the correct structure worked out, you will need to decide what you are going to say. Coming from a design background, it was a real shock to me when I found out that so much of what influences a conversion is down to the words on your website, not the visuals. They say a picture speaks a thousand words, and it certainly can. The problem is; the words are those of your visitors and are open to interpretation. What one visitor sees as inspiring, another may see as dull, what one will take offence to, another will appreciate the 'angle' you have taken.

Pictures are like comedy. They can be very effective communication devices, but if the intended recipient doesn't 'get it', then your message falls flat. Words (or Copy) are the number one conversion medium. Now you have to work out what to put in the words. Knowing that words are the correct device is different from knowing what the individual words should be.

Allow me to shed some light. We have already spoken so much about finding your avatar for best and worst customer. For the prospect you want and the one you don't. Your words will attract some people and repel others. You can't really help this. If you tried, by making your words too Woolly, then that too would attract certain types but really put off others. So, you can't help but to attract and repel at the same time.

This book is not, by the way, a copywriting book. They exist in the bucket loads. You can find 'Direct Response' copy, 'Sales' copy, 'Business' copy and more. You will need to work out which style suits your business in the same way that you worked out a style for your social media communications. However, regardless of style, you have a common objective in line with every other website owner. You need to move a website visitor down the path to becoming a website enquiry or sale.

Before we begin to feel like this could be manipulation, we should go back over how people have arrived at your website and why they may be on your website. If you have done all the correct methods of attraction, the people that are on your website have shown you (by their clicking), that they are interested in finding help with whatever it is you can help them with. To fully understand this, we need a little psychology.

Everything we do, and therefore buy, is to help us between two opposite poles of need or 'feeling'. We have an inbuilt desire to move away from Pain and towards Pleasure. Think about the more recent purchases or actions you made. Uncover the 'desire' underneath everything and you will see this statement is true. Once we see that it is true, the role of your website is to help (or sell to) your website visitor. Remember, selling is helping if done correctly and with the right motive.

So, by the very fact that someone has arrived on your website, they are telling you that they have a need (or desire) to move away from pain or towards pleasure and they believe you may hold at least part of the answer. It is your responsibility to help them. This means making the words as easy for your visitor to understand as possible. Once again, we are walking through their shoes. This means highlighting the benefits of your widget, not the features. Your visitor wants to know whether your widget 'will move them towards what they seek', not necessarily the 'details of how it will do that' at this point.

Just as nobody wants a 13mm drill bit, they want a 13mm hole; your customers are not buying the features of your product or service from you. Trust me on this, they are buying the results of what you do, not the process. If the result moves them closer to their desired position, you have ticked a box and they may just be willing to pay for that!

Let me give a very clear example. In my business, I have learnt a lot about the wider business objectives and why businesses do or at least should exist. I am very passionate about producing a return on investment. It stands to reason then that prospects who believe that a better looking website is the answer to moving them towards their desired position, will not 'buy into' my approach.

On the flip side, business owners who have become frustrated at the lack of performance from their internet activity and spend will really 'buy into' my Return on Investment message. The 'better looking website' feature that we offer and the 'number one in Google' are just features. They do not describe being closer to their desired position, if the desired position is to create financial freedom (pleasure) or stop the business from losing money (pain). As a website visitor, you need to hear (or read) the words that speak of where you are coming from, not simply describing what a company can do.

Features and benefits have been spoken about in marketing for some time now and you may well have come across the subject before. I would say that we need to move things up a level now. Our understanding has gone beyond features and benefits. The forward thinking companies now describe the desired outcome or result that the customer will get by buying the widget. This makes sense. Why leave a gap for the customer to fill in.

Layout

As you describe the results your website visitor will receive should they become a customer, think about the layout of your text and supporting graphics. Reading from a screen is hard enough. Don't make it harder.

There are some basics in terms of font use. Since 'web safe fonts' are limited, you only really have one choice and it is 'Arial' or the Mac equivalent (don't shoot me!!) 'Helvetica'. Let me demonstrate. I have provided the full list of web safe fonts below. Yes, the full list!

Arial

Courier New

Comic Sans

Times New Roman

Before any web guys jump in, I should say that whilst for many years, these truly were your only choices; there are ways now to embed fonts. That said, if you want your fonts to display equally on all browsers; mobile or otherwise, then for the current time, you still have the same four truly web SAFE fonts.

Use white space. This doesn't necessarily mean 'white'; it is a term used to mean empty space. The basic premise is that you allow each element to have space to be easily read. This principle ties in well with not having too many calls to action on a page or too many messages. Keep things very simple. In print terms, you would leave at least 5mm around an item. An item could be an image, a 'stand out' box, a bunch of text and so on. When you do this, you will find the page so much easier to read.

Think about your menus. Do you have a top menu, side menu or both? If you use both, why do you need to? Is it very obvious why? Quite often we don't think through this and end up with poor navigation, which we explored early in this chapter. The same issue can have a negative effect on the overall layout too.

Design has to support the words you use. You will find a very deliberate and common theme throughout this book, my seminars, video's, and interviews; in fact anything that requires me to discuss online success. I do not rate design as highly as I once did; before I learnt the true mechanics behind online success. Whilst I was still a designer who happened to design for web! That said, if your website looks a mess, do not expect people to give your words the time they deserve. You can't build a page that has all the correct messages, technical layout and navigation structure but falls down miserably on design.

Imagine hearing a rave review about a new car. It has excellent fuel consumption yet beats many others on 0-60. It has a lifetime warranty on all parts and labour and qualifies for free road tax. When you enter the showroom, you can see why. It looks like a throwback from Cold War Russia. You may try to justify its lack of beauty, but for most, that will be tough. Now imagine you had entered the same showroom without reading the review. The car salesman tries to hand you a brochure containing the glowing technical (almost miraculous) specification. How keen are you to get over the ugly first impression and find out about what the car could do for you?

You can see then that I do actually believe you need a good looking website. In fact nothing in the rest of my key message goes against this, it just re-prioritises. Design is often the top priority, it isn't; it is _a_ priority. Whilst on this point, equally, do not labour over the design. If your designer presents you with a design that is consistent with your branding and allows easy access to the real content, then what else can you do by changing it? I see this all the time. People spend sometimes days, even weeks, going back and forth changing small details on the design. These minor changes cost money (whether you realise it or not) and do not benefit the business in any way.

Enough on design! Finally, another consideration should be some 'easy links' at the footer of the page. You will see these on many websites. Things like your terms and conditions, privacy statement, sitemap etc are all required, but do not need to take up room on the main navigation. Put them in the footer.

Call to action

What you must put on your pages, is a clear call to action. You have attracted people through all of your 'attraction' work; won them over by your great visual layout and well crafted words, which were easy to navigate to, but now what? You know that the purpose of your website is to get your visitor to take action, but what action should they take if you do not spell it out?

You need to decide up front what stage a visitor will have been taken to by the point they have read your page. From this point, you need to move them on. Think of your call to action as a 'P.T.O.' If you saw this simple acronym (Please Turn Over) on a sheet of paper, you would. Now, what is it that you want your reader to do? I understand there may be lots of options you would be happy with, but be very careful. Offering too many options at this point is dangerous.

Work out the best place to put your call to action too. Consider where your testimonials are going to be (discussed later). Your offer could be well placed next to the testimonials. See on the illustration to the right how Urban Media place the offer in-between testimonials (proof of quality) and blog posts (proof that we are walking the talk)

Think of the 'kid in a sweetie shop' syndrome. If you have raised my interest level and let me know what I can do next, I am more likely to engage with you than if you send me away to decide. You will have to come up with a 'movement' that you feel most people will be happy with. You will also have to be happy to do this in the understanding that the next 'move' could have been bigger for some, but will also be too big for others.

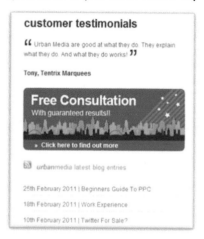

If you think about this properly, your call to action could help to filter out your worst customer avatar. If you need customers that are keen to learn about a subject, let them sign up to your 'guide to' auto responder. If you need customers that can show financial commitment, sell a small item on the site. See if your prospect buys in at an early stage. There are a variety of next step 'call to action' options. Find the one that will work best for you. Test your decision; change it if you need to. Whilst you shouldn't change your site too frequently, do not be afraid to change something that is underperforming. Think about it, what do you have to lose?

Value chain

A single call to action should not be confused with having multiple 'entry' points for your prospects to become customers. I call this, the value chain. You may well have seen this as 'bronze', 'silver' and 'gold' packages.

'Economy', 'Economy plus', 'Business' and 'First class'. These are all ways of allowing people to engage your services at a level they can commit to. I am fully behind this method and you will see it across my businesses.

The call to action is different to value chain. A single call to action may say 'sign up for a trial'. The value chain refers to what fee/service they are signing up to. A typical approach to this should be a page that lists the options in a 'comparison' style, which then leads to seperate 'detail' pages for each service. From these detail pages, the single call to action can relate directly to the service offered on that level of the value chain.

Remember, once a prospect has signed up with you at a certain level, you have the opportunity to demonstrate that at whatever level, you would provide excellent value. However, the higher the level, the more value you provide. This way, a prospect finds their own 'comfort' level to begin the relationship and through providing excellent value and clear demonstration of what else you can do, your client will soon 'up-sell' to another level. Using this method, you will need to get your benefits of each level clear and concise and then over deliver on the expectation.

Testimonials = increased sales

If there was to be a chart of top ten conversion mechanisms, I would vote every time for testimonials. It stands to reason that you have to get the right product/service, but the right product/service to one will be different to another. What will be a great deal to one prospect; will fail to impress a different one. Regardless of 'who' fits the bill of being attracted to your product/service, testimonials will be crucial.

Using testimonials is nothing new. Some industries believe in them more than others, but I don't think there is anyone that is against them. When I talk on this part within my various seminars, I have only ever once had someone say 'what if people don't believe my testimonials?' this is a fair comment, but one that I am not sure is a big concern. I have some ways to make the testimonials more authentic below, but let's just take the comment at face value.

What if your prospects don't believe your testimonials? I would suggest they would also be the type of prospect that wouldn't believe you when you told them it was your 'best price' or that it will take you 'three weeks to deliver' etc. I have found in life that we tend to treat others like we are ourselves. This very simple sentence could help you with the recruitment of customers.

If you have a prospect that does not 'believe' your testimonials, they are showing a high level of mistrust. Why? Do you not assume everyone else is like you until you are proved wrong? I know I certainly do. Despite the fact it has previously tripped me up. It is an inbuilt programme. We don't think about this stuff. Trustworthy people are trusting. Honest people believe others and so on. In the same way, the opposite is true. So before worrying that someone may mistrust your testimonials, have a little think. Is this a problem?

This said, you can help your prospect to believe you. This is quite simple. First, put names, positions, company and dates on your testimonials. Now, I don't want the details to overshadow your testimonial itself, so you may need to decide which bits of info to put with the testimonial. You could also, show the testimonial in both an abbreviated format, but linked to the full version with all the information.

I have a client that didn't want to (different to not allowed to) show this information because a competitor may see who they are working for. Let me cover this one off. If you are really happy with someone and you receive a sales call from another potential supplier of the same service, how keen are you to jump ship? There is a sliding scale here between very happy with the current supplier and therefore would not move, through to unhappy with the supplier and waiting to move.

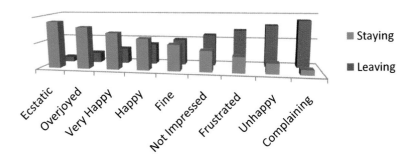

I have a motivational theory that potential 'pain' should be with the person who should be responsible for whatever that potential 'pain' refers to. Let me explain. As a supplier, it is your responsibility to keep your customer happy. If you are not providing value, why should your customer suffer? So taking this slightly further, if you are providing value, then your customer is happy, they will not move. If you are not providing value, they will not be happy, they may move. Anywhere in the scale from one of these to the other, the less value you offer, the more potential for you to feel the 'pain' of losing that customer.

Better than text based testimonials, use video. This is easier than you think. There are plenty of 'flip' type HD cameras on the market that you can use. There are even video testimonial guys that will film them for you. The output quality and the time you have to put into this will affect which method you use, but the point is, there are very inexpensive ways to generate video testimonials. In fact, you could argue that the more professional looking, the less genuine they may appear. You have to decide what works for you. My point here is that video testimonials allow your prospect to see the 'whites of the eyes' of your current customers. This is very powerful.

What's on offer?

I always recommend that you place a well signposted offer on your website. It may be a 30 day free trial; it might be a free consultation. Your offer may be a discounted period or 'cash back' at the end of a period. The details of your offer are not too important. Again, you need to decide what the offer is to make it very relevant to your prospects. Look to other industries. Mobile phones are often sold with a free games console. Why? Because people who like the latest phone; actually like the latest gadgets. If they like the latest gadgets, they will like the latest games console. What is it your prospects would appreciate? In business to business situations, it may have to be a lot more relevant than a games console. Or does it? You decide.

Think about what you can offer that would actually up sell your products/services. Book three training courses, get the fourth free. If this is too much of a stretch to expect a prospect to see added value, what about 2 delegates for the price of one? That wouldn't cost a great deal more. A plumber could offer a free 30 day after installation check on any new boiler fitted. The options are endless. What I can say is that sometimes, we just need that 'push' when we have a decision we want to make anyway.

Remember, we all buy on emotion then justify with logic. Make your offer appeal to the emotion. Silly as it sounds, a meeting in a hotel that your prospects would aspire to go to might be a meeting getter! Imagine call now and I will buy you tea at the Ritz?! Sound silly? Well, maybe it isn't. If you get twice as many appointments, it may be the most cost effective way of managing your pipeline. Be creative and be ready to have a better offer for when your competitors copy you!

Your 100% Satisfaction Guarantee

I love this one. A high percentage of the people I meet actually provide a guarantee. Then when you ask them, they say that they couldn't possibly offer a guarantee. The point is, the concept of a guarantee frightens them. And yet, the practice of providing a guarantee is something they already do. Let's take a look.

If you messed up someone's order, what would you do? Try reading that again, with an emphasis on the word 'you'.

Special offer turns a 'maybe' into a 'no-brainer'

When looking at what had driven the high level of take up of 'Highway CRM', Urban Media found that the 30 day free trial was the number one reason.

The trial had been supported by a 90 day 100% satisfaction guarantee, and this had also affected conversions greatly.

The availability of a 'try before you buy' meant that some of the people interested in the CRM and Automated Marketing solution had moved from a 'maybe' into a 'yes' without further persuasion.

When asked, recent subscribers also pointed to the free product training offer as another deciding factor.

Urban Media looked at the 'cost' of the offers and showed clear evidence that "they were well worth the cost as a 'marketing' expense'.

You see, if you are going to offer the guarantee, you are the one who it refers to. If your customer fails on their part, you do not have to pay out. It is only if you do not do what you said you would, that you have to act on the guarantee. Wouldn't you do that anyway?

The part about if the client messes up, is not and should not be used as a copout either. Be very clear and lean towards being in favour of the client in grey areas. This will teach you to build better processes in the future. At the same time, do not let the variable factor of the client stop you from promoting a guarantee.

Some people struggle with this concept. I believe it is easy for anyone to offer a guarantee. Just look at what you would expect if you were buying the product/service yourself. If you would expect it, chances are your prospects would expect it too and therefore, you should provide it. If you do not, is it fair that they pay? I am hoping you have just said 'no'!

Money Back Guarantee's are the simplest and most clear cut. You will do 'X' or your client gets their money back. If we do not achieve 'Y', you pay nothing (no win, no fee).

Whilst this all sounds very altruistic and this is the only reason you should offer a guarantee, there are some very interesting maths behind offering a guarantee that are firmly stacked in favour of you providing one. Let's say you offer a guarantee. You will gain more business as a result; promise. Now, let's say for every 10 extra pieces of business you gain, 9 are happy and one does take you up on your guarantee. If your gross profit is as low as 10%, you will still make a profit on the decision.

Allow me to expand. 10 customers each spending £1,000; then one customer asks for a refund. You therefore have delivered 10, but only get paid for 9. If you had 10% gross profit, you will receive £9000 in income which covers the cost of your 9 other sales. Not great profit, but what other sales will the 9 lead to? Simple answer; lots!

In reality, you are unlikely to get anyone claiming their money back if you are good at what you do. And even if they did, you will have made a huge additional profit on the 9 that didn't claim their money back on your 'ironclad' guarantee. What's more, if they claim a refund that could be good news too! Not so sure? Well, I would far sooner know that I had a problem rather than all of my customers be unhappy and have a nightmare in the wings just waiting to happen.

One person claiming a refund may be the 'prod' that you needed to look at whether you are offering true value to all of your customers. I am hoping that I have reassured you as to the positives of providing a guarantee. This section is not designed to scare you; in fact the opposite. If you run an honest business, guarantees are your friend. Just make sure that when you offer them, you do not fill the guarantee with lots of 'get outs'.

Equally, asterisk's (*) are banned!! If you need to put a long list of criteria, don't bother. It makes me feel worse, not better. It changes a feeling of providing me with a feeling of 'I trust you' to a feeling of 'you don't trust me'.

Video is the new black

Seriously; in 1998, I started to look at websites as a medium to deliver audio and video. Just think of that. I had started Urban Media to create videos. I wrote cinema adverts! I also quickly knew that the web would end up as a delivery mechanism for more than just web pages. As a result, I began to put more focus on building web pages despite at the time being involved in graphic design, music, video and 3D animation. I was probably ahead of my time, so rather than the 5 years hence that I predicted, it took about 10! The timeframe was wrong, but the theory was right.

Video is now set to take the next stage of the internet forward. Once again, I would recommend that you see where the business sense is. YouTube is the second biggest search engine as I write this; and why? As we discovered in an earlier chapter, YouTube was bought by Google. The reasoning is self perpetuating. Google realised that the search culture would have to grow to include video sites, so it invested heavily in YouTube. Having invested heavily, Google is committed to ensuring the success of YouTube. Not that it needed a leg up in the first place!

So if you accept that video is indeed the new black, what can you do about it? How do you capture this naturally occurring trend and use it to promote your business? You could go out and do a video walkthrough of your offices, but would that be of any interest to your prospects? A factory tour may be, but again, look at your avatar. Would it be of interest to them?

One thing for sure is that we will now go through the process that we have already had with email. The early adopter group contains a lot of 'spammers' whatever the medium. They just seem to not be able to help themselves. There is a void to fill and they can't help filling it with junk!

Your challenge is to be creative and work out what quality video content you could create. If this kind of creativity is simply not your forte, get some help. There will be a lot that you can do. getting some professional creative help may just unblock the creative block and put you on a roll.

Some ideas include;

- Video Testimonials
- Product demonstrations
- Your personal intro to your company
- Interviews with clients as to how they benefit from or use your products or services
- Top tips to help clients use your products better
- 'alternate' uses of your product

And there are lots more uses. The key, is to make sure that whatever you create, it is quality content led. Whilst you need a certain video quality, the content is more important. Just like with your website itself. Remember, the design is important of course, but nowhere near as important as the content.

Advertising on your site (Adsense)

With all of your work attracting potential customers, you will inevitably find some are simply not your ideal prospect or the time is wrong. You should have a mechanism for capturing these people and sending automated marketing where applicable, but what about getting an instant return.

The same Google Adwords Pay per Click that you can pay to advertise with, could also be a source of immediate income. This is possible by putting Google's adverts on your pages. Google call this their content network and it is probably the simplest form of affiliate scheme (discussed in the next section). Quite simply, you place adverts on your website that are relevant to the content of your pages.

As you would expect, there are various controls you can use to ensure correct targeting and block competitor's adverts from showing up. The Google Adsense web pages provide lots of detail on how to get the best out of their system. What I want to do is explain when and how you might use Google Adsense as part of your online success strategy.

Despite the best efforts of the best marketers, you will attract to your website, a large group of interested people, but also, another group of people, but these are not interested in your products or services. This is usual; nothing to be alarmed about. But could you make something on the transaction? With Adsense the answer is yes.

You have to consider the use of Adsense within the rest of your strategy. If you decide that placing Ads within your pages will not distract visitors that would otherwise convert into enquirers and then customers, Adsense could be for you. Here is how it works.

Once you have setup the advert system and built the 'code' into your pages, Google places adverts on your website. Your visitor takes a look at your website and decides the content of the advert is more attractive to them than your website content. This may be ok. Remember, if they are not interested they are probably not your avatar. Either that or your content was always going to struggle to convert them regardless. The visitor clicks and advert and Google charge the advertiser. Out of that charge, you get a cut on the takings.

This Adsense is not for everyone, but before discounting the idea, you should consider whether it is a good way to actually get paid for all of the people that would otherwise not buy from you anyway.

Affiliate Schemes

If you are happy to pass on 'referrals', then installing affiliate schemes on your site may be another great way to generate income from your website. Whilst not necessarily the types of website that I tend to consult on, there are websites that are completely based on residual income from affiliate schemes so what are affiliate schemes?

The most well known website that uses affiliates, we have already mentioned; it is Amazon. Just as you can offer reseller systems to generate traffic to your website, you could also add a revenue stream to your website by being an affiliate of another website; possibly even Amazon! Once again, the principle of using an affiliate program on your website is based on the fact that not all of your visitors are necessarily either ready to spend with you or relevant for you.

Let's use Amazon as the example. You could 'sell' books on your chosen subject from your website within a few clicks. Visitors find you through the various techniques you have used to attract your audience; some of which are just looking for information. Upon reaching your site, they have a quick look around, but a book on the subject catches their eye. They follow the link and buy the book. As a thank you Amazon pay you a commission for delivering the sale. Anyone can sign up to become a reseller or affiliate. This could provide you with a small, but easy residual income.

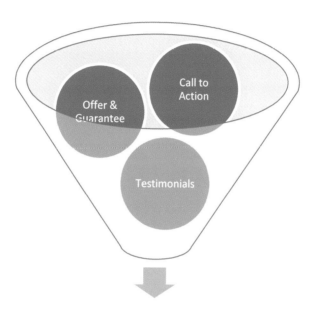

More Conversions!

Quick Recap

- ✓ Make sure your visitors can navigate easily
- ✓ Do not complicate the message
- ✓ Remember, you are writing for your 'Avatar'
- ✓ Selling is helping someone to find what they want
- ✓ Keep the layout simple and clean
- ✓ Design is important, but not *that* important
- ✓ Have one call to action to save procrastination
- ✓ Consider your value chain (bronze, silver, gold)
- ✓ Testimonials are the number one conversion tool
- ✓ Provide an enticing offer
- ✓ Remember we buy on emotion and justify with Logic
- ✓ Guarantee your success with Guarantees
- ✓ Video is this seasons new look but its here to stay
- ✓ Consider placing Google Adsense on your pages
- ✓ Could you generate cash while you sleep through reselling?

After each Chapter, we will have discussed a lot of idea changing topics. They will apply to you differently depending on your exact requirements in relation to budget, industry, approach and more. This page is for you to write any ideas that have come to you whilst reading the last chapter. If it is blank and you have nothing to add, re-read the chapter! This time, think of each section in relation to your business.

Measure

Without measuring your level of success or failure, you will never be able to steer your online marketing activities on to greater things. Sounds obvious, but do you currently know what is happening with your online campaigns? By this, I don't mean how many hits you have had! I mean sensible information that tells you what you need to know in order to keep improving.

Online marketing is a moving target. You aim for improvements, tweak until you get them and then once you have them, aim for new improvements. If ever the phrase 'the only constant is change' were true, it is here. This is why when the snake oil sellers come knocking at your door (usually through spam in your email inbox), do not fall for the 1 upfront fee to get you to number one on Google. I can promise you, this is an ongoing journey.

So, assuming for the minute that you are part of the majority (which of course you may not be!), how can you collect 'intelligence' rather than 'information'. It is actually simpler than it may first seem when you open up Google Analytics or similar. In this chapter we will discuss what you need to understand in order to achieve continual improvement.

In case you have no access to any website statistics currently, let me explain. Website 'stats' refers to data that can be collected about visitors to your website. We will look at what types of data shortly, but to gain access to this data, first you must install some software to collect the information. As I write, Google Analytics is leading the way. It is free and you simply add a piece of code to the bottom of your pages. This is easy for your web developer and they should already know Google Analytics.

Google Analytics

Of course, this is not the only analytics tool, but if you don't have any 'in built' statistics, for example. on your web hosting provision, then I recommend just installing the Google Analytics code. I have spent years being surrounded by the 'anti-Microsoft' brigade; those who feel that when a company becomes successful, you shouldn't allow them the success. I think this will happen to Google too, but think about your business. Google Analytics is probably the best available for the price (zero!) so why would you not use it?! Lesson over!

The kind of information that you can gain is huge;

- Entry Pages (where they entered)
- Exit Pages (where they left)
- Visitor Paths (the journey they took)
- Goal Conversions (visiting pages you choose to be a 'goal')
- Referred Source (where did your visitor come from)
- Visitor Location (where visitors are viewing you from)
- Time on Site (how long are people staying)
- Frequency of Visits (how frequent are visitors coming back)

These are just a few of the ways that you can track data. The funnel feature is also very powerful. This allows you to setup up visitors 'journeys' as funnels in analytics. This way, you can see how many people drop out at each stage. This is not all, but equally this is not a book on Analytics. I just wanted to give you a feel for what you could be finding out if you are not already.

Deciding what is important

With all of this data, it is important that you decide which pieces of information are useful to you. You could easily spend all day just dissecting information. If at the end of the day you do not have any clearer idea as to what you should do next, then it has been of no value to you.

Equally, if you spend all day and the result is you make a change that over the next month generates you £100 in additional sales, could you have had a more guaranteed way of earning that same £100 in less than the day it took to read the data? So, again, with all of this, you have to watch how much time it takes. I am very pro using analytics. I wouldn't have included a chapter on its use if I was not. I just want to remind you again that time is money. It is therefore very important that you decide what is important.

Now, what is important to you may not be important to someone else. An e-commerce site will certainly have very different looking statistics to those of a high price niche market consultant. They should be different. On one, you could be looking for a lot of visits, accepting that a small percentage will buy and you already expect an equal number to click on your Google Adsense adverts. On the other, you expect very few visits. A high percentage though should download your free report.

Using the 2 opposites above, how relevant is number of visits? They are certainly going to be very different in terms of quantity. Gaining high levels for the shop sounds like a great idea. It is less important for the consultants. They should be more interested in conversion rate from visit to downloading the report. This is just a very simple explanation. No doubt you can start to think about what may be important to you.

Assigning Actions & Responsibilities

The challenge for a lot of businesses is that their website is (and should be) so integral to their business. This means that responsibility for making a success of the website falls to a large group of individuals. However, what tends to happen is that one person is given the task of managing the website and the rest look to that person to 'make it happen'.

You need to work out all of the people required to make the website a success. You then need the buy-in from them all. To truly make the site a success, you will need everyone to be involved. Let's say for example that a sales call comes into the office. Doris (a term of endearment in my office!) answers the phone and doesn't quite get round to asking where the caller had heard about your business. The call goes through to a sales guy who quickly realises that the sales call is not a 'perfect' fit for your business and recommends another local supplier.

No problem, you didn't want the sale anyway, so the data is not important. WRONG! Imagine this is repeated three times throughout the month. At the same time you receive three sales calls that are relevant and as soon as the sales person realises, a full 'discovery questionnaire' is completed, where at this point you find out that the caller got your number through your website. Now, from the previous 2 paragraphs, you have three new sales from the website. What else can you tell me?

You can't tell me that half of the sales calls from your website are time wasters, because your team failed to collect that information. If you are to be truly successful, you need to know this stuff. There is a big difference in your requirements based on the data you receive and track.

Or take another scenario where you want to increase the number of customers going to the website so that they can see your new products.

You decide to ask your despatch department to include a postcard in every delivery and ask your customer service staff to mention the website to all the people they talk to. After three months, you have received very few additional visitors. What does this mean?

Well at this point, you don't know. It could mean that your staff didn't have the time to tell people. Maybe your despatch guys simply couldn't be bothered putting the postcards in or maybe the message didn't get through to everyone. It could be that all of your team did as they were supposed to but people still didn't go to the website. These different options have different 'corrective measures'. If your staff are not engaged with what you want to do, you need to incentivise them. If customers are not, you need to incentivise them.

I have used 2 examples, but there are many more. You need to assign actions AND responsibilities. This way, you know what you want done and what you need measured. Google Analytics can track a lot of information, but not everything. A lot of the tracking will be offline too. Once you have decided what is important to your business, you need to measure that information by assigning to the relevant person(s), the correct actions, and also responsibilities.

Bounce rate

It is vital to everything you do, that you are attracting the right people to your website. Simply generating large numbers of visits will not create any lasting online success. For this reason, it is common to look at your 'bounce rate'. This simply means the number of people that land on one of your pages and immediately leave. They effectively come to your site and 'bounce' back to where they came from. Not a problem you may think, but wherever a visitor has come from, they have cost you money.

That may be easily traceable money or it may be opportunity loss money. If you have invested time in using keyphrases that are creating high bounce rates, you are wasting the opportunity. If you had more relevant keyphrases that didn't 'bounce', then you would create more revenue. So, the reverse of this is you are losing money in one way or another while your page is receiving a high bounce rate.

In some scenarios, there are reasons for a high bounce rate. As always, you need to work out what an acceptable level of bounces would be for your website. In very few occasions, bounce rate is actually irrelevant. This is uncommon though. Start with the assumption that you need to keep this low!

Referred source

You will need to know where your visits are coming from.

Bouncing High for kid's toy retailer!

One online retailer explains how his business is bouncing high as a result of using a name similar to one used by a very different online business.

Whilst looking at his website visitor data, he realised that whilst the web sales were flying high, the number of people coming to the site and leaving immediately meant he was also 'bouncing' high.

"This could be seen as a problem" he explained "but we then realised that the people making up our 'bounce rate' were actually looking for a property portal, not our site; 'pricerighthome'. It's an easy mistake to make"!

Once they realised what was happening, they were able to keep an eye on bounce rate, but not carry out any 'corrective' work. They had a justified reason, so they could focus on more relevant data to improve their website.

Why plough money and time into an activity that is not working for you? If you know that you are paying a company to achieve Google listings for you, but you are not getting a high level of visits through Google, you can start to investigate why. If you are getting a lot of visitors coming through some posts you have made on third party blog's and forums, you should do more for example.

You will also get to see which keyphrases were used to send visitors to your pages from search engines. This is useful as being number one in a search engine is only vanity until you start receiving visitors and indeed, visitors that become customers. Using the referred source (and referring keyphrases), you will get to see what combination of adverts, social media activity and natural optimisation is working. You will also easily see what is not.

The 80/20 rule or 'Pareto Law', is as potent here as with any other area of business. Until you start to look at what methods are driving visitors that buy, and which activities are either failing or driving away visitors that do not buy, you will undoubtedly spend 20% of your effort generating 80% of your success. The problem is; because you don't know this, you will also spend the remaining 80% of your effort struggling to ultimately achieve a quarter of the same success.

Visits

When measuring your conversions, you need to understand visits. There are 'hits' which are definitely not visits. There are visits, then there are repeat visits. Either of the latter two are good, but for different reasons. If you have a service or product that requires very little evaluating and is bought once or at least infrequently, then a repeat visit tells you something.

That visitor is struggling to find the information that they need or they are a deliberator! Is this a trend? Are lots of people also 'repeat visiting'? What does this tell you? It could be that you had it wrong in terms of the easy decision making process you believed your prospects went through. It could equally mean, you have not worked out a way to get the prospect the information that they want in an easy to digest format.

Go back to the section on 'copy'. Are your words clear? If they are, and you have tested your belief in this, then can you create tools to help your prospects with the whole decision making process? Certainly for Urban Media, we see a lot of people who want to understand how to be successful online before engaging our services. We run seminars on the subject as a result. We know people are finding it hard to place their investment with a company, so we help them. All backed up with testimonials, offers and guarantees of course. Remember, this is a complete package. Taking one concept out of context will not work.

If you have a high 'visits' count rather than 'repeat visits' count, but you want people to come back to your website regularly, then you are not making the content 'sticky' enough. You are not providing them with sufficient reason to keep coming back. You should then also look at how long people are staying on your site, this may be another enlightening statistic.

Time on Site

Are you building up quality content that you want people to stay on your site for? Videos or slideshows may be a perfect example of this. If so, is the time on site going up. As you continue to build up related content, how much is it being consumed?

It used to be suggested that in order to make a sale you needed to have an average of 7 'touch points' with the prospect. Averages of course are exactly that, but they don't come from nowhere and they are better than finger in the air guesses! More recently, we have heard that we need to be spending 7 hours with a prospect rather than sending 7 items. This is great for all of those corporate hospitality guys. For most companies, taking prospects out is the only way they will be able to spend 7 hours with them. But you can be smarter than that online.

By creating video etc, you will be engaging prospects for increased amounts of time. The way you track this, is by increasing the 'time on site'. As such, this will be a key measurement once you understand what the figure should be for your particular site and more importantly, your business.

Goal conversions

The ultimate reason for all of this effort of course is to achieve 'goals'. A goal in web analytics terms is simply a visitor doing something that you have identified as an action you deem a goal. So what does this mean to you?

Whilst goals vary on each site, they are typically;

- Filled out a contact form
- Downloaded an e-book
- Visited the contact page
- Requested a call back
- Bought a product

You may come up with your own. This list is not designed to be exhaustive, just an idea starter. Within analytics, you can set 'funnels' which are paths towards a goal and 'goals'. Goals are the measure of success as far as web conversions are concerned. Remember though, you may have a phone number prominently placed across all of the pages on your site. Prospects may choose to call rather than filling out a form. In fact, chances are, they will choose to call rather than fill out a form!

Your website conversion rate is measured by taking the number of visitors and the number of goals. How many visitors does it take to create how many 'goals'? This ties directly back to Lifetime customer value. You will know how much each goal is worth, so therefore you can work out how much a visitor is worth.

So although a goal is the 'end' from the online part of the process, it is also the start of the offline for those businesses that do not complete the whole process online.

Summary

Whilst throughout this book, we have seen consistently that each website, each business and each area of a business has different requirements; different online marketing 'settings' if you like. There are also some common threads.

You are trying to generate visits to your website and convert them into paying customers. It is then quite obvious that if you do not have a dashboard, how can you see where you are going and what is working or not working? You need to get to grips with analytics in order to get the most out of everything else. As you do this, keep it simple. Do not over complicate things. This just leads to procrastination. Also, do not have analytics at your fingertips merely to see what has happened. This whole thing is moving. Use analytics to drive forward not look back.

More information to 'steer' with!

Quick Recap

- ✓ Decide what is important to your particular scenario
- ✓ Assign responsibility to the right person for the right task
- ✓ Ensure all of your team are motivated to help measure
- ✓ Keep your 'Key Performance Indicators' simple
- ✓ How did they get to your site?
- ✓ What did they do on your site?
- ✓ How many did what you wanted them to do (Goal!!)?
- ✓ Continually feed the information back into improvements
- ✓ Analytics highlight the past for the benefit of the future

After each Chapter, we will have discussed a lot of idea changing topics. They will apply to you differently depending on your exact requirements in relation to budget, industry, approach and more. This page is for you to write any ideas that have come to you whilst reading the last chapter. If it is blank and you have nothing to add, re-read the chapter! This time, think of each section in relation to your business.

Continued conversations

So, to what I consider the 'new frontier'. The continued conversation is the 'killer method' to online success. And yet, we have already been through how to attract people to your website, how to convert them and how to measure everything that you do. So what is left? What is this 'continued conversation?

You will have seen throughout this book, that the real 'secrets' are in fact not secrets at all. They are obvious ideas that have been around for many years before the internet was ever invented. The way to online success, is the way to offline success. You gain a customer; exceed the expectations of the customer, repeatedly. They refer others to you and spread good words about you, which makes every additional customer easier to gain.

The internet then is just another medium to master in the same way that printing and subsequently telecommunication changed the business world. The 'secret' to success has remained consistent; it is about staying in touch. By staying in touch you can understand what customers want. You can tell them of other products or services that you could provide for them. You can remind them that you still exist!

Given this understanding, who should you spend most of your time speaking to? Well, we have already discussed how most businesses spend 80% of their time and money attracting new business rather than servicing those existing (and more profitable) existing customers. This means, simply by some basic maths, that for every minute you spend talking to your customers, they are hearing four other minutes from your competitors. Maybe it is time to redress the balance.

Easy said, but how do you find the time to continue speaking (in the same quantity/quality) to your prospects and now, really up the game in terms of speaking to your existing customers. After all, let's face it, the existing customer knows you. They won't just leave because you haven't been in touch. Will they? Well, more than you think I'm afraid. Most customers leave through a feeling of 'indifference'. Research shows that whilst some customers leave due to a known problem and others through the contact moving on/business closing/need no longer there, the vast majority just don't feel loved. You didn't talk to them enough.

You need to automate some of these communications. By this, I do not mean spam. I have turned projects down previously through just the slightest mention of a 'list'. Don't get me wrong. You need to develop your database and this could be termed your list. What I refer to is a 'list' that has been bought. There is a whole practise of providing freebies in return for an email address. In fact, I provide content this way and I fully intend to stay in touch through email. After all, if you have liked some of my material, chances are that I have other content you may benefit from. This 'list' is actually my database of people who have found benefit from my internet marketing material. Why would the same people be interested in some get rich quick scheme or quick health gain potion? They wouldn't, so what is the point in someone buying my 'list' to promote their product.

The whole subject of the 'continued conversation' is dependent on a good CRM (Customer Relationship Management) and Automated Marketing system. You will not be able to do everything that you need to do without one. In fact, having an easy to use, yet powerfully featured system is so crucial that I designed my own! I knew that the next step for those businesses that want solid returns from their efforts needed such a system. Throughout this chapter, you will get access to some very powerful ways to stay in touch with your customers and prospects. All of the techniques are made easy within Highway and potentially other systems. Naturally, I am going to talk about how Highway automates the process but this doesn't mean it is the only way these communications can be automated.

Mass Mail is dead (if it ever lived!)

Simply sending out poor quality mass mail to people who may or may not have some vague interest in the 'offer' is in my view, spam. I 100% disapprove of the technique. So we have that out on the table. If you want to build a huge list of random names on the basis of the numbers game, this book has not been for you. Let me give an example that illustrates very graphically my point. Afghanistan is currently an 'issue' as I write this. The 'good' guys are trying to find the 'bad' guys to stop terrorism. Basic view but I am sure you get it. Now, we could just use chemical warfare and kill all living things in Afghanistan. We would surely know that the bad guys were no longer a threat. The problem is, there are lots of good guys in Afghanistan who would suffer as a result.

Is this farfetched from the practise of spamming? Well on one side it is. There are no deaths involved in me opening yet another Viagra, Porn or Gambling site email. This is true. But you should know that email is the number one killer of time for any business. I have been a little heavy handed to demonstrate my point, but it is serious. DO NOT SEND SPAM.

So far I have said that we need to communicate more, and then that we shouldn't send Mass Mail, so what can you do? The correct way to achieve regular communication without spamming is through targeting and speaking to those you know about things they want to know about. To do this, we need to learn what our customers buy from us, need, like etc. we need to build up a relationship.

Email newsletter

The email newsletter has been around for so long that it has become dry. Let me explain why this might be though. You have a long lost friend. Well, they are not lost because every Christmas they send you a note about what they are up to. It is irrelevant to you and after a few years, you mean to read the notes, but at best you skip through. After all, you are very busy and its years since you ever spoke to them.

Whilst you may intend to be interested and you feel maybe you should be. The reality is that you are busy and every day you have to make on the fly decisions as to what you have time to do. That reminds me, that bit of DIY still needs doing! You have no 'active' relationship with them. It's sad, but true. The newsletter is just no longer relevant and as a result, you take no action as a result.

Contrast that with a letter from your close family member living overseas. They are always in touch. You have a good relationship. They send out a quarterly newsletter that is fun and relevant to you as you have a good relationship anyway. The newsletter just adds value to the relationship. You look forward to receiving it because it is always an interesting 'digest' even though, you are regularly in touch anyway.

You can't just use your email newsletter, regardless of frequency as your sole method of keeping in touch. Newsletters without conversation i.e. the ability for the recipient to respond, is an added error here too. So from the 2 'don't do's', we can work out what should be in the newsletter.

When sending an email newsletter, and I suggest you do, make it fresh, relevant and interesting. You can only do that if you understand what your customers want to receive. It is no point me saying; make your newsletter funny, if your recipients wouldn't appreciate the humour.

Using links within the email newsletter that are 'tracked' will give you very accurate information in terms of what your recipients genuinely find interesting.

You need to provide an unsubscribe mechanism, but that should go without saying. Do not be afraid of this. I often find people who would sooner their recipients move their unwanted mail to the 'deleted items' folder than unsubscribe. They fear the 'unsubscribe'. Why? Remember, you want a small responsive audience way more than a large unresponsive one. Once you know what your target audience is, you can be more specific with the message and build far greater response.

Let's say that 80% of your audience wanted a comical Friday afternoon newsletter that took less than 2 minutes to read. The other 20% wanted a more instructive, longer, more serious quarterly. You could keep it halfway and send it every month. Both groups may accept this as it is not what they want, but it is close enough. Wrong! You have just alienated everyone.

In Seth Godin's Tribe talk at TED, he said "who are you upsetting". What he means is that you can't appeal to everyone. This is so true. So you have to decide what your audience wants; be specific. When was the last time you asked? Would it be that radical to send out an email to your intended recipients saying that you want to start a newsletter but only if it would be of benefit to them. Ask; how frequently should I send it? How long should it take to read? Do you want funny or informative or a mix of both? Do you want special 'customer only' offers? Explain that you are doing this because you want to add more value to your existing customers than your 'prospects'. Does that seem all that 'weird'? But I bet you have never received such a survey!

Told/Sold (gap analysis)

One of the problems I see with email newsletters is that companies use them to sell their wares. Is this a problem, you say. I believe so. If I already buy your XYZ Product, then when you try to sell me it again, I feel with good reason, that you never wrote the email for me. Go back to how our communications should be the exact opposite of 'Mass mail', then the scenarios where you send all of your messages to all of your contacts are now banned. You simply cannot send everything to everyone and hope that you will be forgiven. Just as what we say is only 7% the words that we use (the rest being non verbal cues), in the same way, your email speaks as much through what you don't say as what you do say.

If you sell me a product that I already buy, you have just informed me that not only do you not know what I buy, but more worryingly, that you do not care. So when you change the wording to carry a message covering the eventuality e.g. 'if you do not already use XYZ, we would like to demo....' you have not helped. Now you have confirmed to me that you don't know whether I use your product or not. You have also just told those that don't already buy it that you don't know those that do and you have made the problem worse by telling both groups that you don't much care! However you justify this, the best that can be said is that you care about your customers, just not enough to send them only communications that they are interested in.

You now have 2 options. Firstly, you could take the last paragraph and just simply stop mentioning any products or services that you offer. Alternatively, you can get to know what people buy from you, have been told about and whether a product/service is applicable. Imagine a customer that has bought your top of the range product and then receives messages saying that your mid range product is very reliable etc.

They are now wondering why they paid more. Or, the guy who bought your mid range product only to find himself mailed to death with messages letting him know exactly why his mid range product is not good enough!

Let's scrap the first option immediately. All of this talk of getting to know your customer etc. is based on making a financial return. You are carrying out this extra work to improve your return. So if you do the work and then can't send out a sales message, you have defeated the object. Get this section right and it will deliver consistently higher sales and just as importantly; consistently happier customers.

On to option 2 and the work involved seems excessive for the return. You will need a system to automate this for you. As you read the next paragraphs, be aware upfront that there is a way to automate this process. First though, let's explore how you could tell each customer about the specific things that apply to them. This would need to be a personalised message to each individual customer.

If you were to do this monthly, the process would be to keep a list next to each customer that tells you the products/services that they have been told about or sold. You would also need to mark down which products/services are not relevant to them. For most of us, our full range of products and services is wider than a single customer would have need for. The last thing we want to do is to attempt a sale when the product has no relevance to the customer.

Each month you would go through your list of customers, find a new product or service that they have not been told about or bought and of course is relevant to them. Having identified the 'gap', you are now in a position to email the customer with details of your offer.

A lot of work? It is if you need to do this manually and we accept that is the problem with mass mail. Because the work is excessive, a lot of companies just blanket mail us all. This means that the relationship is devalued. But they are working on the ratios that if you sell enough, the devaluing effect is 'collateral damage'. It is not sought after but at the same time, it is accepted.

This book is about internet marketing. Whilst as an

You're Great; We're leaving?!

Web design Agency shocked to hear the words 'you're great but we're leaving'. Unknown, to the agency that prided itself on not being too 'pushy'; the long standing client was about to outgrow them. Whilst this can be a natural thing, it was the reason why that caused confusion.

The company had always provided excellent customer service and through its efforts, their client had achieved a degree of online success. The client just wanted 'more' services.

When asked what they meant by 'more', it was clear that the web agency was already helping other clients with the same requirements.

Throughout the discussion, it became apparent that by being 'non-pushy', the agency had simply failed to keep their client informed of the growing ways in which they could add value.

The 11th hour talks saved the day.

'insider', I can see some of the horrors that the internet has brought, I also see some of the fantastic opportunities. To me the greatest asset of this new media technology is automation. If your CRM (Customer Relationship Management) system is worth its weight, it will not only record information, it will take the legwork out of communication, without depersonalising the communication itself. Highway CRM and Automated Marketing obviously does exactly that. It (like any CRM) contains a list of your customers. It also has a section where you can list all of your products and services. They could actually be any 'message' that you needed to get out. Next to each customer, you can enter whether they have been told or sold the product or service. You can also mark an item as 'not applicable'.

For each message (product/service) you can write an email that will later be personalised with the recipient's name. Each month, the system (e.g. Highway) will go through each customer and tell them about one additional product or service. There are specific copywriting skills to get the best out of these emails, but that would form a whole new book (coming soon in all good bookstores?). What I want to get across in this section is that the process of going through each contact yourself would be huge. Using new media (internet marketing) technology to do this for you provides you with a massive competitive advantage.

Sometimes, the thought of the task can be enough to put you off or simply 'freeze' you as you contemplate 'where to start'. In these times, we need to think about the outcome. If your customer received an email from you each month telling them of a product or service that you could offer them. Bearing in mind that the product or service is of value to them, they don't already buy it from you and you have a great relationship with them, do you think that your sales to that customer would increase? The answer should be YES!!

Auto Responders

I see regular communications in a few different ways. Newsletters are a way that you can talk to the masses on a regular basis. They send the same message to everyone (on the list) on the same day. Told/Sold style gap analysis automation sends a unique (preformatted, but relative to the client at that point in time) message to all of your customers on a one to one basis but again, typically preset on the same day. Sometimes though, email communication should be sent in response to an action. In its most basic sense, if you are away from the office for a week's holiday, what happens when someone emails you? They tend to get an 'out of office' email. Who sends this? It is sent automatically by your email system. You set it up and it does the work for you whilst you are away.

There are a range of circumstances where we can take this very simple example and build on it to automate a series of communications that emulate the conversations we would have anyway if only we had the time. These emails tend to be known as 'Auto responders'. The concept is very simple. Think of the communications that you would send if you were trying to create the perfect customer experience and had all the time in the world. If you have drawn a blank, we will discuss some examples shortly that may get you thinking. Once you have the list, you simply map out the process and write the communications to the particular 'individual' at the particular 'point' they would be in.

Now you have the email sequences written for the wide variety of situations. You could simply save them in a text file and use them later to save a lot of time. The challenge then of course is remembering who should receive which email at what point. Enter once again the need for an automated 'web based' (not reliant on your computer being on or connected to the internet) system. Automated Marketing systems use Auto Responder sequencing to send out pre formatted emails that are personalised and sent out on the right day, based on what has been set by the campaign in terms of delay from the initial email.

There are 2 types of systems. Some let you 'set' the delay of each action by frequency i.e. every day/week/fortnight/month etc. whilst the better systems (Highway!) let's you specify number of days from the initial action. This allows you to set a fully customised sequence. With this flexibility, you could alter the frequency over time so that the sequence of emails changes and does not become too clinical. Remember, this activity whilst automated should feel natural. After all, you are simply automating what you would have otherwise liked to have done if you had the time.

Let me provide an example to help explain how you might use a varied sequence. A visitor to your website picks up on your offer of receiving 'ten things you need to know about widgets. They hand over their name and email address and you send them an email that introduces the first thing they need to know. The next day you send out the following tip and each day a further tip until day 10. Now you could end the sequence there or you could lower the frequency to weekly and send over a following 4 'hidden' considerations that your recipient may want to know. Finally, you may want to send 5 case studies of how people have used your particular brand of widget. You could send these 21 days apart.

You see, at the time that the website visitor entered your website; they had a heightened sense of the requirement. As time goes by, their 'top priority' changes too. By mapping their priority level with your email frequency, you are building rapport. You are staying on their radar without spamming them.

Finally, Auto Responders can be used to filter prospects just as much as they can be used to attract more business. Go back to the thoughts on using your website content and even key phrases within your search engine campaigns to attract and filter at the same time. If say you run a consultancy that charges (with good reason) high rates; then you do not need to be spending time filtering out those that whilst I am sure would like to use your services, in reality can't afford. Using Auto Responders you can provide lots of free valuable content to those people. This

Timely reminder saves customer worry!

It could be said that car garages are not the most pro active internet users, but not so for one local garage that are finding 'web automation' is having a positive effect for their customers and their bottom line.

Using an automated email response system, the garage sets a reminder to be emailed to the customer 11 months after their MOT. This timely reminder not only helps the customer to remember, it secures the business for the smart thinking garage.

This is just part of a 'toolbox' of automated emails that the garage uses to help their customers.

Reminders for winter servicing saw bookings soar as the seasons changed. "We love the emails. They are funny, but useful at the same time. After all, we're very busy and without them would probably forget" said one happy driver.

will in turn spread good word about you and your company. At the same time, by keeping your price structure visible, the Auto Responder is pre qualifying your pipeline.

Mail Blasts

There are other times when you need to 'segment' a group of people and send them an email – fast! Once again, this process should not only be quick and easy to use, it should be recorded somewhere. This should ideally be recorded in the regular notes section of a 'contact record' in your CRM. This way, when you are on the phone to a contact, you can see which automated communications they have received. Once again, if you were to send these emails from your email software (Outlook, Gmail etc) you would then have to manually record the email into all of your recipient's records or simply have no future memory of it.

Summary

There are and indeed should be a range of ways to communicate a variety of messages to your contacts. After all, one size fits all is 'Mass Mail' or as it is known by its real name; spam. You hate spam. You hate feeling that our supplier does not care. Why use the internet to emphasise these feelings for someone else. If you genuinely enjoy the feeling of receiving direct mail that has no relevance to you; or sales literature that attempts to sell you a product you already have, then go ahead and prove me wrong. My guess is you don't like the feeling, but maybe hadn't seen it from the other side in quite such graphic detail.

You should use the communication method that is right for the communication; sounds simple enough. Find your voice within the communications. This is something that you hear a lot about with social media. It is relevant to all of your business communications. How would you speak to a prospect or client in a meeting at your office? Then this is how you should speak to them in email communications. There are 2 potential errors here. The first is to 'downgrade' your language. This is where you speak in shorthand. Text speak would be an exaggerated version of this. The second is where you become a lawyer for the day. Because it is being written down, you think about your words so much more. WHY? If you need to think about what you are saying more than during a verbal communication, I would suggest you need to think more during those too!

I said at the beginning that I would speak of automation from the Highway point of view as it is the system I designed. This doesn't mean to say it is the only system, but what I would say is make sure that you can do everything from one package. You don't need to be importing and exporting data all day. This doesn't help you to gain competitive advantage and that is what automation should do. Your offline communication should be informed by your online communications and vice versa.

To do this, the communications that you automate are communications that you would have carried out anyway. You are simply using this automation to save you the time that you already don't have.

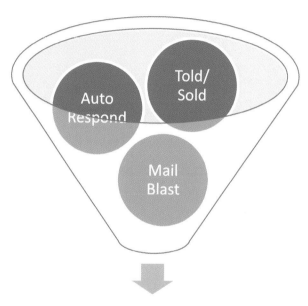

More Satisfied Customer Sales!

Quick Recap

- ✓ Online Success 'Nirvana' is a result of continued conversation
- ✓ If you are not talking to your existing customers, who is?
- ✓ Don't raise your voice! Talk as you would in a meeting
- ✓ Existing customers are more profitable
- ✓ Spend 80% of your 'marketing' time on Existing Customers
- ✓ Spend 20% of your 'marketing' time on New Customers
- ✓ Automate as much as possible
- ✓ Auto Responders can be used as much to filter as to attract
- ✓ Use 'Told/Sold to continually cross sell to happy customers
- ✓ Use Auto Responders to provide relevant value driven content
- ✓ Use Newsletters to build community feel
- ✓ Use Mail Blasts to tell 'specific' contacts something fast
- ✓ Record everything in your notes section for each contact
- ✓ Track everything important
- ✓ Web based (Cloud) systems are online all the time

After each Chapter, we will have discussed a lot of idea changing topics. They will apply to you differently depending on your exact requirements in relation to budget, industry, approach and more. This page is for you to write any ideas that have come to you whilst reading the last chapter. If it is blank and you have nothing to add, re-read the chapter! This time, think of each section in relation to your business.

Appointing a partner

Before we discuss the 'how to' appoint a partner, I guess we should explore the fact that you need to appoint one. Now the last sentence deliberately avoided the question of whether you need to so let me explain.

Your Car; who does the work on it when the MOT comes up each year? For those of us that are in the first 3 years where there is no MOT, who services the car?

Your Accounts; who files your annual returns? Who carries out your tax computations? For growing companies, this will certainly include; who does your book keeping?

Your legal battles; who created your terms of business? Who would you use to fight off any legal action? Or pursue a debtor?

Now, if you do all of the tasks above yourself, you may not get this section. To give you the benefit of the doubt, there could be one of two reasons for this.

1. You are a control freak (not an accusation, just a question?!)
2. You haven't realised how valuable your time is

If it is the first option, this book will not change your mind. You will need to take the wealth of information with you as you read through the more detailed 'how to' books on the particular specialist subjects.

If (and I hope), the reason is that you haven't realised quite how valuable you are, then allow me to explain. We all have specific roles to do. When we try to do everything, we strangle growth. Now, I have heard people say that they do not want to grow. They intend staying as a 'sole trader'.

They fear taking on people so much that they would avoid it like the plague. This means they need to outsource more, not less! Either way, if you are driving the business or even just the marketing, you can't afford to spend your time studying and staying up to date with the very latest Social Media site or Natural Optimisation technique. You must pass out this type of work.

Isolate what it is exactly that you should be doing. If you are a 'driver', then you need to be well informed about the top level and allow others who cost the business less to do the actual 'work'. Whilst we talk about 'cost the business less', allow me to expand this. You are worth your expected output for your business, not your hourly rate. A business can't operate by charging out your time at what the business pays for it. This means if you are expected to achieve an average of £400/day and you work 8 hours, you are 'worth' £50/hour to the business. The fact that you are only paid £15 is irrelevant. And before you go looking for a raise, the business has a lot of other costs in-between the £15 and £50! There are once again other books that help you to get paid more. This is not one of those.

If you consider that it will take you twice as long to carry out an activity e.g. optimise your own web page; this would be a very conservative estimate. This means that you could outsource the work for up to £100/hour and it still makes sense. This is with one small addition. If you do not use the 'gained' time effectively, then it is just a cost to you. You need to ensure that the time you have is used effectively. This means that when you outsource, you gain more time to use effectively and find ways to increase the return on your own time. Also, you do not have to pay £100/hour for someone to do the 'doing' work.

Accepting that you are in agreement that it makes sense to outsource the actual work involved in building your online success; then you need to be a bit wise as to how you select your partner. This doesn't mean finding the cheapest. Remember, the whole book is about return on investment. This should drive your selection process.

Cost and Expectations

Just as often as I see horror stories of 'bad developers' charging ridiculous prices (low and high), I also see clients with unrealistic expectations. So, how do you know what to expect when outsourcing a website build is not exactly an everyday occurrence?

First, this is going to be a partnership. You can try to 'screw the guy down on price', but he will just 'screw you down on service'. He will leave the situation feeling bad about you and you will feel bad about him. And the benefits to both of you are???

From the outset, look for a partner. This means you need to assess whether you can work with them. I have introduced the term 'them' and will expand this shortly. Before you even look at their case studies, be honest; could you see yourself going down the pub with them? This doesn't mean you will, but the most successful websites have a very successful relationship behind them. We for one, recruit our clients based on this! If we can't 'work with you' then we don't want to 'work for you'. It's nothing offensive; just we know what the success ingredients are. I guess what we are really saying is 'can you trust them'. Also, did they get it? Whatever the project is, they need to share your excitement. Now you can't expect them to be quite as passionate, but you will soon see whether this is just another project to them or whether they really want to be involved.

Next, look at their team. I have to be upfront and apologise to the 'one man bands' at this point. I have been there and I know what it is like. The reality for you as a business though is that you need a collection of specialists on your side. The guy who can design your brochure and your website, build online applications, optimise your pages for Google and manage your Twitter account is being over ambitious. I know this sounds a little harsh, but I see it all too often. This is a path to limited success at best.

The skills needed to be good at design are 'creative' or 'right brain', for those that understand some basic psychology. The skills needed for the serious web build stuff are very mathematical or logical. This is 'logic' based or 'left brain'. The skills needed for an internet marketer are I guess more a mix of the two, but even here, they are not far enough to either side to be great at the other two roles. And this is just at its most basic. We could then look at what interests your team. You need a mix. Let's look at a full service law firm. The 'family' law department do not do 'traffic offences' or even 'litigation'. The accountancy firm will have a 'M & A's' (Mergers and Acquisitions) specialist alongside 'book keeping', 'Tax Specialists' and general 'business accounts'. The minute they need to offer financial advice, they go outside their experts to get even more professional help.

The internet is not IT by the way! This is another expectation that you should have (or not have). When you take on a team of internet specialists, that's what they are. Even in my brothers company, they call up my guys with computer problems; we are not IT!

Meet the team. Find out that they are real. You will need to ensure that you have specialists working together. You need to know that your 'team' do not care how much of the work is social media or how much is building complicated online applications. They just want to provide the most effective solution to drive your success.

In order to do that, you will need to provide the correct content at the correct time. Quite often, as a client, you know that you need a website but you don't know what to put on the site. This is fairly normal. You start building up an idea of 'home', 'about us', 'services' and so on. Having read this book, you will have realised that you have to think differently about this, but you still have the daunting task of working out what to say on the site. Your team should be able to help. What they won't be able to do is do the work for you. In fact, if they say that they can, alarm bells should ring. Think about it. You are specialists at what you do. How can

I want it all and I want it now!

Having worked with a large company for some time on a variety of Brands and with fantastic results, the time came for the redevelopment of the main company website.

Being honest proved to be the deal breaker when an 'outside' agency took the bold move of promising that they could deliver the new site in 5 weeks and provide all of the content. Seeing the time saving benefit the naive company took the easy option; after all, the offer was too good to reject.

2 years on and without a new website or the intended results, it was time to move on from the hollow promise and realise the massive opportunity loss that the 'short cut' had produced.

The lesson goes to show that more often than not, the best results come from genuine effort. If it seems too good to be true, chances are; it is too good to be true.

another company be specialists at what you do and at what they do? It doesn't sound right and it isn't right. Walk away if the company say that they can take that hassle away. The only guarantee you have here is that it is coming back to bite you!

What you should expect is help. Whilst you are the experts in your field, they are experts in theirs. Whilst on the subject, if the design looks good, leave it. Moving that 'logo to the right a bit' will make zero difference to your bottom line and it is the first sign that you are focusing on the wrong stuff. That doesn't mean if the site looks average it is ok; not at all. You need good design as part of your overall requirement. I am simply saying that going into the finer points of the design are where hours are lost and nothing is won.

Allow me a quick common sense observation whilst on the subject of time. If your team have allowed 10 hours for a design and its hour 20 and you are messing around with 'silly' stuff, where do you think the other hours are coming from? Forgive me for being honest, but they are not coming from your teams 'spare time'. By the way, your team will of course never tell you this. You will be having time shaved back from other activities. So being specific will help you all to come up with the right visual look and feel first time and then providing the content in the right format at the right time will also help you both to achieve the success that you both want.

On the subject of content; I have seen it happen so often that you start to send through content in sections because you feel it helps the developers. Halfway through section 3, you realise you need to update a previous page so you send that through again. Not a problem surely; it's only copy and paste. Not so; the simple copy and paste in Word may not be the same in HTML. Then, once the copy and paste issue has been considered, what about version control? By the end of the website build, you are frustrated that the web guy has incorrect content on the page and he really shouldn't have because you have sent it all through numerous times. And there you have it; the simple phrase 'numerous times'.

You can see how so much of the site success is down to both sides of the team, the client and the supplier. Like anything in computing; garbage in – garbage out. You need some structure to the process. Look for a team who will enforce this. It isn't a bad thing that they are restricting you. See it as a cuddle, not a noose! A good team will have proper processes in place that allow a degree of flexibility, but have boundaries; boundaries that are designed to help you succeed.

Finally, what can you expect to pay? This is more difficult. There are good teams and bad teams. Whilst the phrase 'you get what you pay for' is generally accurate, I have seen web companies charging excessive prices and getting away with it up until the point that the client realises they have not benefitted from the work done. On the other hand, I have seen companies charging too low prices and eventually they go out of business or have to hike the prices up. The one thing I can say is that price should be low down on the checklist. This does not mean prepare your open cheque book. It means that you should be looking for return on investment.

If I had a company that turned every pound I gave them into 2, I would give them all my money. If I had another that turned that same pound into a pound (or less), I wouldn't give them anything at all. This seems fair but I still see companies basing their investment on price. It appears to be built into us. I can understand on commodity items but appointing a web team is far from that. To get a better idea of what to pay, you need to look at the company's testimonials and guarantees. If they have a powerful guarantee, that is one thing, if they have a stream of glowing testimonials, that's even better. Look out too for those who offer the phone numbers of existing clients. We often have clients offering to be contacted by our prospective clients. They want to sing our praises. Your web team should have the same.

Their testimonials

What a testimonial says will tell you a lot about the company. You should match your requirement to their testimonial. If you are still looking for a 'pretty' website, you need to seek out the testimonials that say how creative a company is. If you are looking to turn your website into a cash generator, look for testimonials that speak of success and return on investment.

Also, if an agency comes in with more visuals than testimonials, walk away. Seriously, walk away. They are more interested in their design than your success. There are lots of adverts on TV that win awards but fail to drive new business to their owners. Do not fall into that trap. It will only impress you until your budget has been spent and you have not received a return.

Look at testimonials in relation to the size of company that relates to you. A company that works well with Micro businesses may not be suitable for medium sized companies. Your web team need to understand your specific needs. Having said that, weigh this up against all the other factors. How important is it to you? If it is very relevant, look for the types of companies that the web team have worked for. You can go too far of course. I have been asked before to demonstrate that I have 'done this before' in specific terms and of course that I shouldn't be currently working with any 'competitor'. So that means we have failed a previous company doing the same thing right?

Their guarantee

A company that offers a guarantee is one that knows what they do will work. Look out though. A company should only guarantee the things that they can be fully responsible for. For example;

Bad Guarantee

We will get you to the top of Google for a one off payment; guaranteed!

Look at this for a minute. First of all, there is no ongoing relationship. Once you have paid your money, the recipient has no reason to stick around. Secondly, if the guarantee is not from Google, then it is irresponsible. If the result can't be guaranteed (and in this case, only Google could guarantee it) then the writer of the guarantee has to be questioned.

Good Guarantee

Try our new service for 90 days and if you are not entirely satisfied, we will give you your money back!

There is no argument here. If you are not entirely satisfied is something that only you can say. If you claim your money back, how can it be questioned? There is also a time limit. The person offering this has considered the implications. They know that any genuine person would know within three months whether they were getting good value for money. Also, the guarantee states what will happen.

I hear so often; do this and I guarantee you will get this. 'Cut out carbs (carbohydrates) and I guarantee that you will lose 2 stone'. Ok, and if I don't, what then. Make sure any guarantees you are offered are clear.

Also, if there is any small print, it is not a guarantee. It is the ramblings of someone who daren't offer a guarantee but knows they should really?!

Summary

You should get a 'feel' for the right partner. Just to make sure you are not being 'sold a line' though, have a checklist. You are recruiting a partner after all. Read the Quick Recap on the following page and use this as a checklist for choosing or reviewing your existing supplier.

Quick Recap

- ✓ You NEED a partner

- ✓ Your partner should be a <u>team</u> of specialists

- ✓ Can you work with them; know/like/trust them

- ✓ Don't screw them down on price

- ✓ If a designer walks in to your first meeting with 'designs'; RUN!

- ✓ Don't sweat the small stuff, remember the goal

- ✓ Provide content once and on time

- ✓ Web guys can help but not originate your content

- ✓ Look for testimonials, lots and related to your requirement

- ✓ Look for return on investment/results in testimonials

- ✓ Take up references, good teams have 'raving fan' clients

- ✓ What guarantees are in place?

After each Chapter, we will have discussed a lot of idea changing topics. They will apply to you differently depending on your exact requirements in relation to budget, industry, approach and more. This page is for you to write any ideas that have come to you whilst reading the last chapter. If it is blank and you have nothing to add, re-read the chapter! This time, think of each section in relation to your business.

The Beginning....

If your mind is buzzing with all the things you could do to improve the effectiveness of your internet marketing, I'd like to help!

Urban Media Quickstart is perfect for those who are just getting to grips with internet marketing and need a 'kick start' to create a successful website and Internet Marketing Strategy.

Quickstart is valued at over £2,000 in training material alone!

- Monthly video updates and interviews
- 'How To' video training
- The stuff that wouldn't fit in this book!
- Monthly goal setting plan
- Attend Urban Media 'The Lock In' (Live or Webinar)

You can get all of this through a low cost monthly subscription to Urban Media Quickstart for **only £47 per month.**

Simply go to **www.urbanmedia.co.uk/Quickstart** to get started.

THE LOCK IN

In this full day event, you will get access to our Internet Marketers who will take all of the learning's from this book along with their own years of experience and apply them to your specific website. Hosted by me, but supported by my team; you bring along your login details etc. and together, we will make big positive changes towards your internet marketing success. Whether it is mastering LinkedIn, Google Analytics, or setting up Pay per Click, not only will we help you with the practical steps, we will advise on the relevance and effectiveness for your particular business.

As a result, you will leave with a tailored plan of action and more importantly, the confidence to take the 'Massive Action' required. Since you will have already taken steps on the day; continuing to achieve success online will be easy for you to accomplish. What's more, you will see that sometimes, **Massive Action** doesn't have to mean **Massive Time** required! We will teach you to be smart with your online marketing activity.

Remember, we have limited places on each 'Lock In' so that you get maximum attention. Book your place now!

This full day event, valued at £495 is available to you for only £275. Call 01494 538441 or email direct@urbanmedia.co.uk to book.

Both offers carry a full 100% satisfaction guarantee. **You will be completely happy,** but just to ensure this decision is totally **RISK FREE**; if you do not feel these offers represent excellent value, let me know and get all your money back!

A few testimonials!

After all, if you don't walk the talk.....

Tony Silver FCMI

Top qualities: Great Results, Expert, Creative

"I first met Elton last year when I attended one of his Seminars and was very impressed with the event and the way he communicated with the audience. I have since met him on several occasions and his passion for his company and his products shines through. I have taken one of his products onboard and I am very happy I did as his support is tremendous. If you have yet to have the pleasure of meeting Elton then I suggest that you change that in 2011. Great guy and a great company"

Angus Grady

Top qualities: Great Results, Personable, Expert

"Elton has consistently provided us with great advice and input. He and Urban Media have an ability to cut through the nonsense and start talking about solution led strategies straight away. If you don't waste their time Elton won't waste yours. I wouldn't hesitate to recommend Elton and his team. First class."

Pauline Trew

"Elton & his staff are always a joy to work with. Their humour, sense of fun and yet their professionalism means that they produce exciting websites that will promote anyone's business. They do what they do well, on time and are honest. I recommend using them for any web work you need."

Ian Thomas

Top qualities: Great Results, Expert, Creative

"Elton and his team offer a superlative service from concept to design and continued advice on web design and marketing. If you want to promote your services via the web you need to talk to Elton and Urban Media"

Sally Anthony

"I recently attended Internet Marketing: The Breakthrough Seminar, Elton is a dynamic speaker and I found it really informative and motivational. I highly recommend finding more about Highway and Urban Media. I'm amazed Elton finds time to be such an active person in helping the local community, for instance by mentoring young people. It is a reflection of his energy and commitment to helping others achieve success."

Jay Blake

Top qualities: Personable, Expert, High Integrity

"They only allowed me THREE attributes - that's just not fair! Elton is a top bloke - one who I love working with and who helps me achieve what I am looking to achieve with my business. I have and will continue to recommend that people work with the team at Urban Media. There are many web people that I know but only few that I recommend and he is one of them."

Ceri-Jane Hackling

"Elton is a great person to know and to do business with. He's very supportive, helpful and an all round good guy! His company also designs great websites... Elton is someone that everyone should know!"

Jamie Dunn

"I underwent a Consultancy task at Urban Media as part of my NEA Course. I found Elton to be a great Leader, and somebody that strives to get the best out of people. He always went out of his way to say good morning to be, and this made me feel valued as part of his Company. He also gave me a great Master class in SEO and Website Creation and the tips given on that day have put me in a great position and taught me a lot about Setting up Websites. I would Highly Recommend Elton to anybody."

Shona King

"I've known Elton for a number of years now and have always found him to be an extremely professional individual with a great passion for what he does, be that his work or his trucking! He has presented at various events and exhibitions I've been to and has always given those in attendance, a little something which they can take back to their businesses to help them improve. He's also a great networker and I'd be happy to refer him to business contacts of my own."

Anthony Lloyd

Top qualities: Great Results, Expert, High Integrity

"Elton and his team have been driving our SEO. We are beginning to achieve some excellent results. They are accessible and responsive and I have no hesitation but to recommend them."

Bill Tulloch

"I have known Elton for a number of years and would have no problem in recommending him or his company Urban Media. Elton is not only excellent at internet marketing and website design he is also a businessman who understands the needs and demands of his clients."

Anthony Warren

"Elton has been a leader in local supply of web services for many years. He is also very personable and easy to deal with."

Chris Bourke

Top qualities: Personable, Expert, Creative

"I have known Elton for a number of years and I have always been impressed with his enthusiasm and determination to deliver a top class service to his clients."

Natalie Rice

"I met Elton at a promotional golf day, although I have not used his company's services. I have based my review on the fact that he was a genuine nice person to spend time with whilst working on promotions. I feel very confident that his professional yet fun personality would follow in to his work. I am a big fan of 'people buy people'."

Linda Chafer

Top qualities: Personable, Good Value, High Integrity

"Elton is extremely helpful and very considerate to others. He is understanding and patient with others less fortunate than himself and will take their problems into account when dealing with them on personal or business issues."

James Moorcroft

"Having known Elton for many years since we were in the same business club, then on the committee together, I consider him to be a skilful and dedicated businessman offering a good value great quality product (sorry I can't say you look after my website - if I didn't use a specialist provider that gives loads of technical content, I'm sure I would!)."

Michael van Noorden

"I met Elton through a mutual Networking Group. Both our companies are in the same space with some overlap but we don't compete. I was very impressed by Elton's professional approach and positive attitude. He is direct and honest and doesn't waste people's time. If he can do a quality job or alternatively recommend others he does so and in the latter case - expects nothing in return. I have passed a few lukewarm opportunities his way and they have been actioned immediately. He has done the same for my company. Elton and I meet up regularly at a number of local network groups and he's always got some good news to share and is always willing to help and discuss new ways of winning business. I can recommend Elton as a great business contact."

John Welburn

"Elton has just talked to our Refer-On business Hub at Burnham. He clearly and logically showed us that web strategy is not and should not be a one trick pony. I admire such clarity of delivery. Talk to him and be amazed. It is simple not difficult, just listen to Elton."

Sally Hindmarch (nee Hollander)

Top qualities: Great Results, Expert, High Integrity

"Elton and his team walk the talk! They are consistently helpful, thoughtful and personify customer service. I would happily recommend Urban Media to any of my contacts!"

PJ van Zetten

"In the time I have known Elton I have recognised him to be dynamic, focused, ethical, motivated and amusing - a dynamite combination for a dynamite company. I would have no hesitation in recommending him."

Peter Hollingsworth

Top qualities: Great Results, Personable, Creative

"Elton and his team at Urban Media did an outstanding job on both my company's website and that of a networking group that I help to organise. Elton is a great enthusiast and is totally devoted to delivering customer service."

Malcolm Hill

Top qualities: Great Results, Personable, Expert

"Elton and his team have been, and are responsible for my website from initial conception through to the most important follow up work to drive enquires to our site. Without doubt our level of enquires have increased since Urban Media have been managing our account."

Hilda Stearn

"Elton is determined to help young people to succeed in business - his support for the Diploma programme is well-known (have a look at his website for the podcast!). He applies this same passion to his core business and visiting his offices and talking to his staff it is clear that he leads an enthusiastic team! Some key attributes; passionate, focussed, transparent and committed to helping today's and tomorrow's entrepreneurs to grow!"

Robert Dallas

"I worked with Elton collaboratively on a sizeable web project delivering virtual products through an ecommerce platform. Elton is an extremely talented businessman and an exceptional marketer. He is passionate about his vocation and a great character to work with. I am happy to recommend him!"

David Dorey

"Elton is a great client to work for, he takes time to understand the issues, is decisive and a no nonsense problem solver. Urban Media were one of my largest clients in terms of number of client websites hosted by our company and were adding new business at an enviable rate. I would recommend Elton's services even though I am now in direct competition with him. He runs the second best Web Development Company in the region!"

Peter Henry

"In working to develop a new 'style of virtual company, I have come to recognise that Elton has the ability to get quickly to the nub of any issue."

Sharon Hewitt

Top qualities: Personable, Expert, High Integrity

"Elton has a fantastic knowledge with regard to the Internet and how businesses make money from it. More important than that, he has ability to communicate this in a way that the technophobic person (like me) can relate to and understand. I have no hesitation in recommending Elton to business owners who need expert guidance in web design or indeed in marketing in general."

Steve Hanks

"Very impressed with Elton's ability to offer focused value added solutions to website design and SEO strategies"

Abbey Crawford
Top qualities: Great Results, Personable, High Integrity

"I have worked with Elton and his team for several years and wouldn't change it for the world. They understand return on investment. I know for every pound I spend with them, they will maximise the return."

Katie Banks
Top qualities: Great Results, Personable, Expert

"Elton was a great person to work with as he gave new and innovative ideas when [we] needed to revamp their website. He communicated in a clear, effective way that ensured I fully understood the value he was adding to the project. The end result was a brilliant, patient friendly, new website that had a clear ROI."

Coming soon.....

You
"After reading Elton's book, I took his advice and also enrolled on the 'Urban Media Quickstart' programme. Step by step, I implemented the things Elton and his team taught me and now my website has turned from being a black hole of an expense into a systemised cash generator!"

Thank you

Of course, no man is an island and I certainly couldn't receive regular testimonials like the ones you have just read without my team at Urban Media. Since the team is ever growing and the chances are that I may not keep updating this page!, I will simply say a huge thank you to all of my team. You are the best.

To the clients that allow Urban Media to continue providing excellent value and to my team here at Urban Media who think mediocre is over rated and continue to strive to be better; a massive thank you.

Whilst I have been writing this book, Angela has had to put up with me being very tired as I continued the 'day job' and fitted the book writing around helping others. Thank you, you're ace!!

And of course to those that are proof reading and just getting to this bit and thinking; how come we don't get a thank you?! Thank you for agreeing to read and learn. If you are feeling better educated, then this book has worked. Your feedback has been valued; thank you!

Elton Boocock

You can keep up with Elton or book him to speak at your event through: www.eltonboocock.com